J Forsyth Ingram

The Story of an African City

J Forsyth Ingram

The Story of an African City

ISBN/EAN: 9783744753241

Printed in Europe, USA, Canada, Australia, Japan

Cover: Foto ©ninafisch / pixelio.de

More available books at **www.hansebooks.com**

THE STORY OF AN AFRICAN CITY.

DEDICATION.

This work, on the rise and progress of Maritzburg, is dedicated by the Worshipful the Mayor and Town Council of the City to

HIS HONOUR SIR MICHAEL HENRY GALLWEY, Q.C., K.C.M.G.,

Administrator of the Government and Chief Justice of the Colony of Natal,

As a slight mark of the esteem and respect which his long and useful career as a Legislator, a Judge, and a Citizen has impressed on the hearts of his fellow-colonists.

Town Office,
  May, 1898.

His Honour Sir Michael Henry Gallwey, Q.C., K.C.M.G.
(Chief Justice of Natal).

THE STORY
OF
AN AFRICAN CITY.

Multa quoque et bella passus, dum conderet urbem.

BY

J. FORSYTH INGRAM,

Author of " The Colony of Natal," " Natalia," " The Land of Gold, Diamonds, and Ivory," etc., etc., etc.

All Rights Reserved.

PUBLISHED BY C. COESTER, MARITZBURG.

Printed by Wm. Watson, "Times of Natal," Maritzburg, Natal.

1898.

Cr. J. J. Chapman, J.P.

G. J. Macfarlane, J.P. (Mayor).

Cr. C. G. Levy, J.P.

Dr. J. F. Allen
Boro. Health Officer).

E. M. Greene, M.L.A.
(City Solicitor).

S. Stranack, J.P.
(Town Clerk).

T. W. Woodhouse, J.P.
(Deputy Mayor).

D. F. Forsyth, B.A.
(Borough Accountant).

Cr. R. Mason, J.P.

Cr. P. F. Payn, J.P.

Cr. W. E. Bale, J.P.

Cr. B. S. Kelly.

Cr. B. Ireland.

Cr. W. H. Buchanan.

Cr. T. Raymond.

Cr. W. J. O'Brien.

Cr. R. F. Morcom.

Cr. W. S. Crart.

Cr. C. W. B. Scott.

Cr. S. J. Mason.

CONTENTS.

PART I.

CHAPTER I.—Difference between British and African History—Duty of the rising generation 3

CHAPTER II.—The *dramatis personæ*.—The Stage—A Word Picture of the Wilderness—Chaka's Hosts—Lieutenants Farewell and King—The Zulu Power—Cession of the Territory to the British—Death of Chaka—Dingaan... ... 7

CHAPTER III.—The Boers.—Their reason for leaving the Cape Colony—A Pioneer Expedition into Natal—The Great Trek—Arrival on the Berg—Entering Natal—Negotiations with Dingaan—The Fatal Treaty 13

CHAPTER IV.—The Great Place of Dingaan—A Word Picture—Retief and his Party—Dingaan's Treachery—The Massacre of Retief and Party—Attacking the Emigrants—The Slaughter at Weenen—Relief Columns—The Covenant—Defeat of Dingaan—Bojesman's Randt—The Founding of the City—Its Price in Human Lives—Election of a Volksraad—Naming the City—The Fulfilment of the Covenant ... 18

CHAPTER V.—Arrival of British Troops—Rising Clouds—Withdrawal of Troops—Hoisting of Dutch Flag—The Republic of Natalia—A Peep at the Voortrekkers—The laying out of the City—Troubles at Dingaan's Kraal—Umpanda and followers join the Boers—Defeat, exile, and death of Dingaan—Umpanda declared King of the Zulus 24

CHAPTER VI.—More trouble with the British—Re-occupation of Natal—War—Boer Victories—Steady advance of the British—Submission of the Boers—The Union Jack hoisted and Fort Napier established—Natal a Province of the Cape—British Apathy—An Impossible Position—A new Exodus—Causes which led to the foundation of the Transvaal Republic 29

CHAPTER VII—Advent of the Emigrants—First Municipal Board City divided into Wards—A Retrospect 35

CHAPTER VIII.—Sir George Grey—The Royal Charter—Opening of the First Parliament—Maritzburg declared the Capital of the Colony 39

PART II.

CHAPTER IX.—A Bird's-eye View of the City—Altitudes—Scenery—Contrasts—Fort Napier—Latitude—Longtitude—The Railway Station 41

CHAPTER X.—Municipal History—The first Journals—The first Town Board—The Borough Endowment—The Borough Seal—Parks—Schools—Rash Speculation—Trade Depression—Effect of the Discovery of Diamonds 48

CHAPTER XI.—Preparations for the Zulu War—Maritzburg Fortified—The Boer War—Trade Depression—Effect of Gold Discoveries—Excitement—Wild Speculation—Financial Disasters—Recovery—Steady Progress 59

CHAPTER XII.—Borough Finances 67

CHAPTER XIII.—Public Buildings 73

CHAPTER XIV.—Institutions and Industries 82

CHAPTER XV.—Maritzburg as a Health Resort—Vital Statistics—Effect of Climate on Diseases.—Pleasure Resorts ... 97

CHAPTER XVI.—Education Statistics—Mr Robert Russell.—Maritzburg College—Blenheim School—Girls' Collegiate School—Thanet House School—Murchiston School ... 113

CHAPTER XVII.—Sport in the City—Racing—Athletics—Field Sports 156

CHAPTER XVIII.—Conclusion—A Word Picture—The Opening of the First Parliament under the new Constitution—The Past and Present—Her Majesty's Jubilee—Poem—The Last Scene... 160

Personal Notes 165

Members for the City (Illustrated) 167

BUSINESS REVIEW—Early Trade—Mr. Barter's Book—The Ubiquitous Auctioneer—Boer Vernuckers—Trade Established—Messrs. Mowat & Still—Messrs. Brady & Wyles—Messrs. Collins and Munro—Mr. J. Hughes—Mr. Henry Collins—Messrs. Jesse Smith & Son—Messrs. David Whitelaw and Son—Messrs. Merryweather & Sons—Messrs. R. McAlister & Sons—Mr. John Hardy—Mr. D. Nicolson—Messrs. Turner & Company—Mr. Thomas Hannah—Mr. Robert Fuller—Messrs. P. Henwood, Son, Soutter and Company—Messrs. Clifford and Smith—Messrs. Mason & Broadbent—Messrs Taylor & Fowler—Mr J. C. Baumann—Imperial Hotel—Messrs. W. H. Walker and Co.—Messrs. Schwake, Watt & Co.—List of Mayors of Pietermaritzburg—Cab Stands and Cab Fares—Jinricksha Stands and Fares.

INDEX TO ADVERTISEMENTS.

EDUCATIONAL ESTABLISHMENTS.

	PAGE.
Michaelhouse	iii.
St. Anne's Diocesan College	iii.
Pietermaritzburg High School for Girls	xiii.
St. Charles's Grammar School	xv.
Convent of the Holy Family	xv.
Hilton College	xiii.

HOTELS AND CLUBS.

Imperial Hotel	xliii.
C. Woodhouse	xli.
Victoria Hotel	xlii.
The Grosvenor	xxxii.
Castle Hotel (Howick)	xix
Howick Falls Hotel	x.

MERCHANTS, BOOT AND SHOE WAREHOUSES, OUTFITTERS, DRAPERS, &c., GENERAL DEALERS.

Ireland & Co.	i.
W. Rogerson	ii.
J. Raw & Co.	viii.
Robert Guy	xxix.
Harvey, Greenacre & Co.	xxiii.
Simmer, Jenkins & Co.	xviii.
Mallett & Co.	v.
R. Elliot	xxxix.
A. Ogilvie	v.
E. G. Mendenhall	v.
Taylor & Fowler	iv.
Williams & Lambert	xii.
City Public Supply Stores (Alf. Grix)	ix.
James & Son	xxxv.
Robert Jones (Howick	xxix.

MILLINERS.

Mme. Hamer-Calvert	ix.

CHEMISTS AND DRUGGISTS.

Robt. Fuller	xliv.
Hessey Allanson	xxvi.
Stantial & Allerston	xxvii.

NURSERYMEN, FLORISTS, AND SEEDSMEN.

G. H. Wilkinson	xxxix
Fisher, Prior & Weddell	xl
W. J. Bell	xxv

FURNITURE DEALERS AND MANUFACTURERS.

Clifford & Smith	vii
Simmer, Jenkins & Co.	xviii
John Hughes	xliv

BUTCHERS.

Thompson & Sons	xxviii

SWORN TRANSLATOR.

Mr. John M. Hershensohnn	xl

PREFACE.

—:o:—

The present volume constitutes perhaps the first attempt that has yet been made to publish, as an illustrated work, the history of the rise and progress of one of the pioneer cities of the British Empire in South Africa.

Next to Cape Town, Maritzburg can justly claim to rank high amongst the historically interesting centres of civilisation on the southern portion of this continent, and though lacking the glamour begotten of gold and diamond mines, the City, as the scene of many political and warlike events, has a history which is well worthy of preservation and remembrance.

As the mother City of South-eastern Africa, she has borne her full share in the development of British enterprise in the country, notwithstanding the many grievous drawbacks which have hampered her advancement.

Her citizen soldiers were among the very first in the history of the British Empire to take the field as an organised force against the barbarians, in defence of hearth and home, and her tribute in blood on the field of battle is heavier than that of almost any other town in South Africa.

During two important wars she has been the base of military operations, while as the centre of an agricultural and pastoral district, her citizens have done good service in fostering those important pursuits.

The chapter dealing with educational matters will fully demonstrate the fact that the Government, the Municipality, and the citizens have spared neither effort nor expense in their successful endeavours to supply scholastic advantages of the highest and most approved standard, and to make Maritzburg desirable in every particular from an academic point of view.

It will also be shown that as a health and pleasure resort Maritzburg occupies no second-rate position, and the chapter on the subject will have a wide and special interest to medical and general readers throughout the world.

The illustrations constitute in themselves a fairly complete pictorial history of the progress of the City and of some of those who have laboured for its benefit.

In conclusion, the writer has to gratefully acknowledge the assistance rendered him in the compilation of historical facts by the officials of the Colonial Secretary's office, and many other friends, and particularly by Mr. D. F. Forsyth, B.A., the Borough Accountant, in connection with the financial affairs of the City.

J. F. I.

Maritzburg, 14th April, 1898.

PART I.

CHAPTER 1.

Difference between British and African History.—Duty of the rising generation.

TO write the Story of an African City is a vastly different matter to penning in orthodox guide book fashion the records of one of the stone villages in the country of the Great White Queen across the ocean.

In dealing with almost any of the populous centres of Great Britain, the writer must look to antiquity to furnish him with that picquant dash which lends flavour and interest to his narrative.

The facts he has to chronicle, while perhaps stirring enough in themselves, are oftentimes so remote as almost to have lost immediate human interest.

Very different, however, is it when the historian is called to deal with the events which cluster around the foundation of a city in the wilds of Africa.

MIDDLE UMGENI.

The courage, endurance, and determination which have to be exercised day and night, year in year out, by the daring pioneers of African civilization are subjects well worthy, not only of the pen of the author and the poet, but of the admiration of those whose high privilege it is to be the immediate successors of champions and heroes.

This work is to be no mere recapitulation of dry facts or wearisome statistics. It is the story of men's lives spent bravely and generously in the cause of advancement and civilisation.

To quote the words of a poet :—

"He must be brave who dares the wilderness,
Who breaks the spell of loneliness, and cleaves
A pathway through the wilds, and founds a home
In unknown places."

Such were the men whose lives and works have gone before us, and whose brave example should be emulated. The rising generation of Maritzburg has every reason to be honestly proud of the city of its birth or adoption, and he is indeed unworthy of his heritage who does not resolve to strain every nerve to push forward to completion the great work which, but sixty years ago, was so nobly commenced.

Year by year new and stately buildings are being erected, the town is rapidly taking its place as one of the commercial and educational centres of Greater Britain, its natural features eminently lend themselves to expansion, and given the enthusiasm on the part of its present citizens that marked the career of those of the past, it is difficult indeed to set a limit to the bounds of that progress, the beginning of which is to be recorded within the covers of this volume.

It is safe to say that but few persons in Maritzburg have ever accorded to the history of the City more than a passing thought, and yet the subject teems with interest.

Those who join us will find the reality of history as exciting and adventurous as the most exacting appetite can desire. Before we get down to the period of paved streets and settled homes we must pass, in imagination, through the pathless wilds with the trek Boers, and hear again, in fancy, the rattling volleys from the laager walls and the war yells of desperate barbarians. We must pass reverently by

A FOREST SCENE.

the graves of those whose lives constitute the foundations of the Colony, which now looks to the present and rising generations for its honour and its life; and as the milestones of the years are viewed there cannot fail to rise in each true heart an earnest resolve to be worthy of the traditions and the glory of the past.

CHAPTER II.

The *dramatis personæ.*—The Stage.—A Word Picture of the Wilderness.—Chaka's Hosts.—Lieutenants Farewell and King.—The Zulu Power.—Cession of the Territory to the British.—Death of Chaka.—Dingaan.

THE *dramatis personæ* who are about to play their parts in this story consist of three classes, namely, the Natives, a few adventurous Britishers, and, later on, a considerable company of Dutch voortrekkers.

The time is about 1820.

The stage upon which they are to appear is no mere painted one. It is backed by a grand panorama of rocky mountains, snow-clad and cloud-capped, which trend in a long irregular line from the south to the north-eastward.

The middle distance is made up of open, grassy mountains, black forests, and foaming rivers; while the foreground consists of palms, yellow strand, and ocean. Of footlights there are none, for the play goes on for ever—lighted by day with a sun like a blazing shield, and by night with a glorious moon. By way of music, this magnificent theatre is filled with the sound of the sighing wind or roaring tempest. The songs of birds are hushed now and again by the deep voice of the lion or the hoof-batter of a passing herd of deer. Fair flowers stud the hills with bright points of colour, and the whole scene breathes of primæval peace—a peace which, alas, is destined to be speedily disturbed; for, ere its beauty has been fully realised, the deep-toned chant of a savage war party, swelling in measured cadence as it approaches, proclaims that, even here, the evil passions of human nature are in full play.

The war hosts of Chaka, the Zulu King, are on the march, slaughtering and ravening like hungry wolves;

while their helpless victims, the peaceable tribes of the country, in vain fly for shelter to the cliffs and the forests.

Well may those cliffs and forests reek with blood, and the voices of nature be silenced, for as the hosts sweep on beyond our ken, upon the stage, so lately calm and pure, are seen the ghastly forms of slaughtered men and maids.

Watch that place where the lifeless ones are lying, for on that very spot is destined, when the scene is changed, to rise that African City whose story we are telling.

ZULUS FIGHTING.

While the foregoing scene was being enacted, a very different one was taking place a few hundred miles to the southward on the eastern frontier of the Cape Colony.

Two British officers, Lieutenants Farewell and King, were listening with deepest attention to the stories told them by certain traders and hunters. These latter, who had just returned from a journey through the territory, now known as Natal, were recounting their adventures and travels.

The land was described, and truthfully by them, as a veritable hunter's Eden, and the listeners were sportsmen. The result was that these gallant officers, accompanied by certain friends, set sail for Natal on board the schooner *Salisbury* in 1824, and so enter upon the scene the second set of characters.

At this time, Chaka, the King of the Zulus, was in the zenith of his power and glory, and the nation over which he ruled had become a dominant one, throughout South-eastern

DEATH BY THE SPEAR.

Africa, holding sovereign rights over the territory extending from Delagoa Bay, in the north-east, to St. John's River, and even beyond it, in the south.

The newcomers settled at the Bay of Natal, and at once commenced their negotiations with Chaka for territorial rights, which they obtained in 1828.

It may be contended by some that the foregoing has no connection with the history of Maritzburg; but as a matter of fact it has, for in the first place, had the British settlers not been in firm and legal possession of the Bay and Harbour, it is more than probable that many of the Dutch emigrants, who entered the country shortly afterwards, would have, by preference, established themselves there. In the second place, the treaty with Chaka, signed on the 17th September, 1828, irrevocably ceded to the British a territory extending one hundred miles inland from the sea,

A VICTIM.

so that the site of Maritzburg, though afterwards illegally annexed by the Boers, was fully thirty miles inside the then recognised British frontier.

The British settlers apportioned the Coast-lands out among themselves, and set quietly to work to make the wilderness blossom and bring forth.

Gradually they gathered about them a few scattered remnants of the defeated tribes, and as time went on they became a distinct power in the land. There is ample evidence that they made themselves intimately acquainted with the hinterland of their new territory, but they have, unfortunately, left us scant record of their adventures and sport.

It is now time to introduce the third group of characters, but before doing so, it may be necessary to mention that in the year 1828, and within a very short period of the ceding

HERD OF CATTLE.

of Natal to the British, the Zulu King, Chaka, perished by assassination at the hands of his brothers Dingaan and Mahlangana.

Dingaan having put some of his brothers and other accomplices to death, assumed sovereignty over the Zulu nation, and then set out on a course of extermination against the settlers. His efforts, as far as the British at the Bay were concerned, proved abortive, but alas, he succeeded, as will be shown further on, in effecting terrific disasters on the newcomers.

RIVER SCENE.

CHAPTER III.

The Boers.—Their reason for leaving the Cape Colony.—A Pioneer Expedition into Natal.—The Great Trek.—Arrival on the Berg.—Entering Natal.—Negotiations with Dingaan.—The Fatal Treaty.

IT would be unfair to bring the third group of our *dramatis personæ* upon the stage where they have to play so important a part, without a few words of explanation. For some years previous to the Kafir war of 1834 in the Cape Colony, the Dutch settlers in that country had been

DEAD BUFFALO.

excessively discontented with the attitude assumed by the British Government in connection with the control of the native population.

The events which immediately followed the war brought matters to a crisis.

The authorities regarded the prevalence of a system of forced native labour as slavery, which indeed it was, and terminated it by proclamation at a time when, it is asserted, the farmers stood most in need of harvesting assistance.

It was consequently resolved by the Dutch colonists that an expedition should be sent to explore the countries to the north-eastward of the Cape Colony, with a view to the establishment of an independent state there. Accordingly, fourteen wagons were prepared at Uitenhage, and a party led by Pieter and Jacobus Uys, Hans de Lange, Stephanus Maritz, and Gert Rudolph made their way along the eastern slopes of the Drakensberg, until they finally arrived, to the great surprise of the British settlers, at Port Natal.

DEAD GIRAFFE.

After spending a pleasant time, and learning all they could about the country, they returned whence they came and made a favourable report to their compatriots.

In the following year another detachment of Boers, under Pieter Retief and Hendrick Potgieter, succeeded in finding a practicable pass through the Drakensberg Mountains, entering Natal from the westward.

We have now the third party that is to take a part in the founding of the African City fairly in view, and stirring indeed are the scenes which are about to be enacted.

As the sun arose to lighten the vast theatre which we have already described, and as its rays caught the crests of the rocky mountains which form the background of the stage, a strange and wonderful spectacle is presented.

Away up against the misty sky line, clouds of dust can be faintly seen, and then growing slowly into sight, hundreds

RHINOCEROS.

of lumbering wagons advance over the roadless heights. There, full in sight amongst the cliffs and peaks of the Berg, stand the famous Voortrekkers.

Gallantly have they fought their way over the wilderness, where the hosts of foemen held sway. Time and again have they met them in battle and hurled them from their path, and now, like the Israelites of old, they stand in view of their promised land.

Here, indeed, are the veritable founders of the African City which will shortly rise solid and secure, cemented with the blood which has been shed already, and that which, alas, has yet to be poured out from many a hopeful heart.

Stern Calvanists and fatalists as they were, tinged with the enthusiasm of their Huguenot, and the phlegm of their Dutch ancestors, they regarded themselves as God's chosen

KAFIR KRAAL.

people, who were destined to possess the land, and to smite the Natives hip and thigh.

Wonderfully indeed had they been preserved thus far on their way ; yet might the moralist draw from their subsequent career a telling lesson on the vanity of human hopes Though they stood upon the threshold of their heritage, and looked down into a land which veritably flowed with milk and honey, and which they fondly imagined they had but to go in and possess without further toil, there was yet an invisible barrier of anguish and death which must be passed before they could enter into the enjoyment of rest.

Stretching far along the crests of the mountains, their flocks and herds were allowed to graze while the caravan halted, and a party of trusty pioneers rode down the mountain side to spy out the land. Shortly after, the Berg was swarming with moving caravans as the whole expedition trekked down the slopes intent on taking possession of their new estate.

Well would it have been for them had they patiently waited the development of events, for, shortly afterwards, the most of them were massacred, and the page of Africa's history so deeply stained with blood as to remain for all time a memory of sorrow and disaster.

Scattering themselves along the banks of the Tugela and Bushman's Rivers, they each selected their farms and set about the establishment of new homes.

Meanwhile, Retief commenced negotiations with King Dingaan for territorial rights. Ignoring the British Charter previously granted by Chaka, that wily potentate cheerfully issued another; but, as events proved, without the slightest intention of making it good.

CHAPTER IV.

The Great Place of Dingaan.—A Word Picture.—Retief and his Party.—Dingaan's Treachery.—The Massacre of Retief and Party.—Attacking the Emigrants.—The Slaugther at Weenen.—Relief Columns.—The Covenant.—Defeat of Dingaan.—Bosjesman's Randt.—The Founding of the City.—Its Price in Human Lives.—Election of a Volksraad.—Naming the City.—The Fulfilment of the Covenant.

THE tragic events which are now about to be chronicled have such an important bearing on South African history generally, and Natalian history particularly, that they cannot be lightly passed over.

Far up to the eastward of where the Voortrekkers have made their homes, on the banks of the River Umfolosi, in the territory of King Dingaan, there appears through the early morning light a vast assemblage of Native huts, clustered round an enclosure, wherein stand placidly dosing the household cattle of the Zulu King; for this is the great place of Dingaan.

There appears to be a suppressed air of excitement abroad. Groups of warriors with trailing plumes pass to and fro, while others in dense masses still slumber on the open spaces between the huts. Close by, encamped in a thicket lies the gallant Retief and his comrades.

For weeks the King has kept them in suspense; burning to return to their people, they were resolved not to do so until they could take with them the cession of the territory of Natal, duly attested by the King.

Task after task had been set them to perform; they had cheerfully complied with every requirement of the savages, and now waited but to officially bid the King farewell.

AFRICANDERS AT HOME.

As the morning advanced the kraal gates were opened, and the cattle driven forth, to be replaced ere long by masses of armed warriors.

In due course the King appeared, and summoning the pioneers to his presence, he begged them as a proof of their confidence in his good faith to lay aside their weapons.

This they did, and there, in the centre of a vast horde of armed barbarians, stood the advance guard of Natal's civilization.

With a friendly smile the King stoops forward and lays his hand on the pen which traces his mark or signature; then, calling to the attendants, he bids them bring beer, so that his guests might partake of a stirrup cup previous to their departure. Still with a friendly aspect he raises the vessel to his lips and then passes it to Retief.

VOORTREKKERS' HUT.

Savages as are the spectators, there is a hush amongst them, and the human strain that lies deep in every breast, however criminal, must have thrilled as they waited for the cruel order which was to be the signal for a massacre. The last Voortrekker has partaken and the vessels are carried away. There is a moment's silence, then the King rises calmly from his seat, his eye glances at the sea of waiting faces, his lips pronounce the words of doom : "Slay the evil ones—the wizards!" and the awful work is done.

The slaughter having once commenced, no time is lost in following it up.

That night a great war party set out on its mission of death.

Meanwhile the settlers, unconscious of impending harm, were quietly leading their pastoral lives. Most of the men were away buffalo hunting, while those who remained were so scattered as to be practically defenceless against the terrific rush that was made on them.

After devastating the outlying homesteads the army of Dingaan, flushed with victory and the lust of blood, swept on to the main laager of the Voortrekkers at Bushman's River.

These latter having been forewarned were prepared for the onslaught; and again the curtain rises on a terrible scene of carnage.

War without mercy, war to extermination was the order of the day.

Hedged in by spears and yelling hosts the tiny laager stood the shock. A ceaseless roar of musketry rent the air; frail women and young girls joined the fray; the guns were discharged until they were too hot to load, when they were clubbed and crashed into the skulls of the invading foe.

Four times they charged and four times were they repulsed, until baffled and defeated the savages took to flight.

Within one short week over 600 men, women, and children perished by the spear.

Many of the Voortrekkers were still to the westward of the Berg, but when they heard of the disasters which had befallen their countrymen, a column, 350 strong, was formed, and, under the leadership of Piet Uys and Henry Potgieter, set out to the rescue (in the month of April, 1838) while

Maritz remained behind with the balance of the emigrants. The result, after many vicissitudes, was defeat and disaster to the Boers.

Another column, this time under the leadership of Andries Pretorius, set forth. Prior to starting a solemn service was held by the Voortrekkers, and a covenant made

A NATAL ZULU CHIEF.

with the Lord to the effect that if He would vouchsafe them the victory over the Zulus, a house would be raised to the glory of His Great Name, and the day of the victory be observed by them and their descendants as a holy day for all time. That victory was accorded them on Sunday, the 16th December, 1838.

Having crushed the power of Dingaan, they marched back to their laager in triumph.

Selecting a long, low ridge, named Bosjesman's Randt, under the Zwaartkop Mountain (and, as already stated, well within the bounds of the territory ceded to the British by Chaka), they founded and established the African City whose story this is.

Before the first stone was laid, however, the fights which have already been chronicled had cost over 800 European and between 8,000 and 10,000 African lives.

DUTCH REFORMED CHURCH.

In the latter part of 1838 the Settlement of Maritzburg consisted of six small hovels and many wagons and tents.

In the beginning of 1839 a Volksraad, or Council of the People, was elected, and on the 15th February of the same year, the town that was to be, was officially named Pieter Maritzburg, in honour of Pieter Retief and Gert Maritz.

Fresh caravans came pouring into the country from the Cape Colony, and the actors upon our stage might be numbered by the thousand.

The menace of war had now apparently passed away, and the hill which a few years before had been studded with the ghastly forms of slaughtered savages, now echoed with the laughter of children and the clangour of church bells.

The Voortrekkers had kept their covenant, and built a house of worship to the honour and glory of God.

Such is the story of the founding of an African City.

CHAPTER V.

Arrival of British Troops.—Rising Clouds.—Withdrawal of Troops.—Hoisting of Dutch Flag.—The Republic of Natalia.—A Peep at the Voortrekkers.—The laying-out of the City.—Troubles at Dingaan's Kraal.—Umpanda and followers join the Boers.—Defeat, exile, and death of Dingaan. Umpanda declared King of the Zulus.

ALTHOUGH the actual founding of the City had become an accomplished fact, its troubles and those of its founders were by no means ended.

On the victorious return of the commando, an unpleasant surprise awaited the champions, who had, as they imagined, won, by right of conquest, all the territory which lay between the Drakensberg and the sea.

Whilst the Boers had been engaged in daily conflict with the natives, word had been conveyed to the Cape Colony of the dire straits in which they were placed. As the Cape authorities still regarded them, notwithstanding their protests, as British subjects, Sir George Napier, the then Governor, sent troops forward to put a stop to the war. The detachment, which consisted of 100 men of the 72nd Highlanders and the Royal Artillery, was under the command of

The Story of an African City.

Major Charteris, who was accompanied, as diplomatic agent, by Mr. (afterwards Sir) Theophilus Shepstone, a gentleman who was destined from this date forward to play an important part in subsequent events.

Great was the indignation of the emigrants when they learned of the action of Great Britain.

Finding that hostilities were practically at an end, Major Charteris, accompanied by Mr. Shepstone, after declaring his instructions to the Volksraad, left overland for the Cape.

Captain Jervis, who was left in charge of the British Garrison at the Bay, found the Voortrekkers, both in his own vicinity and in Maritzburg, in no mood to submit to his authority.

On the Christmas Day of 1839 the British Government, having resolved not to colonise Natal, withdrew their troops.

Again the curtain rises on an important period. This time confined to the Market Square of Maritzburg.

As the light streams over the scene, it reveals a few scattered hovels. Wagons are outspanned here and there, while tents of every description form canvas streets to right and left.

In the centre of the scene a tall flagstaff had been erected. Here, there, and everywhere amongst the dwellings and the tents, mounted on their rough but hardy horses, ride the valiant Voortrekkers. Unkempt as their steeds, with flowing hair and straggling beards, clad in fustian garments, slouch hats, and veldtschoons, they presented more the appearance of brigands and freebooters then decent farmers and fathers of families.

The whole scene bristles with rifles. Stalking amongst their masters are hundreds of skin-clad and feather-bedecked Natives and Hottentots.

These are the serfs, bondsmen, and slaves of the emigrants. The morning meal over, the whole population pours out to the Market Square.

First a gallant cavalcade of mounted men, hardy desert rangers, who need no martial music or tinsel pomp to brace them for the fray or the senate.

Close behind them come the mass of non-combatants. Clustering around the flagstaff, where stands their leader,

GRANITE BLOCKS, MIDDLE UMGENI.

Andries Pretorius, they watch him, while he binds on the new-born flag to the halyards. A flash of colour, a roaring cheer, and the tricolour soars aloft. The Republic is born, the new Republic of Natalia.

Considering that the withdrawal of the British troops meant the abandonment by Great Britain of all pretentions to sovereign rights over the territory, they felt that at last they had obtained complete independence.

The gathering breaks up, and the scene gradually blends into one of placid agricultural progress.

New houses spring up in every direction.

The grassy slopes of Bosjesman's Randt are laid out in streets, and the town divided into building lots, 460 of which were sold at prices ranging from £4 to £7 10s. each. By

NATIVE CHIEFTAIN HOLDING HIS COURT.

virtue of a certain regulation, each emigrant was entitled to two farms in the country, as well as a free erf in the township.

Although Dingaan had in the previous campaign been defeated, he had by no means been crushed, and shortly after the hoisting of the Republican flag he began intriguing again.

He had, however, trouble enough at his own court to deter him from active hostilities. His brother, Umpanda, had for some time shown signs of revolt, and at length, followed by fully half of the Zulu nation, came over in a mass to the Boers.

Three hundred and fifty of these latter, at the head of Umpanda's army, set out on a final expedition against the hated King, who was now thoroughly defeated and driven into exile.

Falling back on Swaziland, he was captured by the King of that country, who tortured him to death.

Umpanda was now declared King of the Zulus, and in his gratitude to his Dutch friends he presented them with 40,000 head of cattle, which doubtless he had taken from Dingaan's herds.

As the close of the last chapter saw the City of Maritzburg founded, so the close of this one brings it to that stage when it becomes the capital of a Dutch Republic, whose legislators are not only simple farmers, but valiant pioneers, dictators to vast Native population, king makers and breakers, and sad, alas, to relate, oppressors and enslavers of the subject races of the country.

CHAPTER VI.

More trouble with the British.—Re-occupation of Natal.—War.—Boer Victories.—Steady advance of the British.—Submission of the Boers.—The Union Jack hoisted and Fort Napier established.—Natal a Province of the Cape.—British apathy.—An impossible position.—A new exodus.—Causes which led to the foundation of the Transvaal Republic.

THE Dutch being now monarchs of all they surveyed, the hated British far over the seas, and the equally detested Dingaan mouldering in his grave, there lurked but one poison drop in their cup of happiness, and that was their non-recognition as an independent state by Great Britain.

In response to a communication from them, the Governor of the Cape, acting under instructions from Home, repeated his claim to authority over them as British subjects, which indeed they were.

KARKLOOF FALLS.

For about two years the matter was confined to occasional exchanges of despatches, and no active steps were taken by the Home Government to enforce its claim.

Encouraged by this apathy, it is alleged the Boers commenced a system of oppression towards the Natives.

On an appeal from these people for protection, a detachment of troops under Captain Smith was despatched overland from the Cape.

On the 2nd December, 1841, a proclamation was issued by Sir George Napier, announcing the re-occupation of Natal by the British.

It does not fall within the scope of this work to chronicle in detail the events of the British-Boer war which followed; suffice to say, that several battles were fought, in which the Boers had their share of success.

RIVER SCENE.

On one occasion, ten Britishers were captured by them at the Bay, and brought to Maritzburg in chains, where they were exhibited in public places like wild beasts.

The result of the war was that the Boer flag was hauled down, the newly-established Republic became a memory of the past, the Union Jack of Great Britain was planted on a hill commanding the town, where a fort was built and named after Sir George Napier, the then Governor of the Cape.

Natal was now British territory, and by proclamation declared a province of the Cape. Strange to say, no steps were taken to give effect to this proclamation for some considerable time. Captain (now Major) Smith was nominally head of the province, but the Boer Volksraad lingered on,

THE DRAKENSBERG.

and the Boers themselves at Maritzburg and elsewhere throughout the country, although they had made official submission to the British, were living practically in open revolt.

At this distance of time it is possible to fully gauge the importance to the whole of South Africa of the events which were then about to take place,

The smouldering discontent against the British, of which Maritzburg was the centre, was about to cause the birth of a new Republic, further to the north, of such dazzling brilliance as to attract the attention of the whole civilised world, and to materially add to the wealth of the human race, while at the same time it was destined to be for many years a bar to the progress of the country as a whole.

Dissatisfied at British delay and indifference to their urgent requirements, a number of the founders of Maritzburg once again turned their eyes longingly to the far off wilds beyond the Vaal River.

Failing to obtain the redress they required, which lay in the direction of a recognition of preposterous land claims and rights over the Natives, the settlers again resolved to take their destinies in their own hands, and carve out for themselves an ideal state, where the devil, in the shape of a Briton, might never enter.

Once more the curtain rises on our stage. The time but five years later than the occasion of the hoisting of the Republican flag.

The foreground of the scene remains as it was before, an azure Bay, a yellow strand, a few scattered houses constituting a British settlement.

Further back on the scene is the City, but no longer mistress of a Republic.

The Union Jack floats bravely from the staff whereon had hung the Republican tricolour.

From Fort Napier the frowning guns look down on the sullen town, while under their bent brows dark glances of hate are hurled back by the burghers. No rosy light beats on the silent City, dark clouds overhang it, and muttered threats are heard,

The Market Square is no longer filled with the laughing voices of children. The great lumbering wagons are once more in sight, heavily laden for the road.

Another exodus is taking place, and once again the founders of the City are about to move out in quest of pastures new.

GORDON FALLS.

Now and then, when the faces of the burghers relaxed at softer memories, the glimpse of a red tunic over the ramparts of Fort Napier would set the tide of feeling going, and turning to the caravan, which was to gather strength as it passed through the uplands, they moved slowly away, bearing with them as they went the darksome clouds of discontent and danger.

Though many have gone, many remain, and lo! the scene is brightening with the removal of the elements of discord.

As the founders of the City pass out of sight and enter on their new arena of endeavour, we would be less than human did we not, while fully recognising their shortcomings, bestow upon them the laurels which they have so nobly won. Had they but had patience and knowledge enough to wait the due course of events, many unpleasant pages of African history need never have been written. But this was not to be.

In the all-wise ruling of Providence, and in the Mighty System, which ever works out for human good, the mystery of which no man may solve, it would indeed appear that these simple clans were led by an invisible pillar of cloud and fire through the wilderness, nay, through the valley of the shadow to the green pastures, where they now repose.

Bon voyage, brave hearts, we may meet again; but not on this stage, where Britain reigns supreme.

CHAPTER VII.

Advent of the Emigrants.—First Municipal Board.—City divided into Wards.—A Retrospect.

THE closing scene of the last chapter witnessed the departure from the stage of a large number of its most prominent actors, while the present one is destined to treat of the advent of a company about 5,000 strong to take their places.

Hitherto the bright blue ocean, which bounds the sea front of our Natalian stage, had been but rarely ploughed by labouring keels.

Now ship after ship with spreading sails cleaves her way from the far-off Homeland, each one bearing expectant throngs of emigrants, each emigrant brimful of hope.

In those old days no stately floating palaces with pulsating engines scoured the seas. Bluff in the bows and broad

RIVER SCENE.

in the beam, with stunsail and topsail and royal set, the wooden walls of Britain bore her sons through every clime, and built up many a Power. So was it with Natal.

See there, the *Betta*, the *Sovereign*, the *Conquering Hero*, and a host of others draw near the shore and discharge their living freights.

Hark to the ringing cheers, as the mariners bid Godspeed to the gallant emigrants as they leave the vessels' sides.

Watch the silver spray splash up as the rowers bend to their work, and the boats fly over the hissing bar, and win the sought-for strand.

New blood and new life are in the land, and the wheels of progress move swiftly on.

MARKET SQUARE.

The Market Place of the African City now resounds with the familiar tongues of Lancashire and Yorkshire, Norfolk and Wales, Aberdeen and Glasgow.

The German accent and Irish brogue can now be heard chaffering in the market and the store, while the guttural taal of the Boer still holds its own, for the representatives of the original founders have by no means vanished.

The new epoch gleams bright with promise.

Four years later, when the curtain rises again on the scene, a marked change is perceptible.

The germ planted by the Voortrekkers, and sanctified by the sacrifice of thousands of lives, has now put forth its leaves.

A Municipal Board has been elected.

The City has been divided into wards, and the period of romance and danger has been replaced by one of established law and order.

MARKET SQUARE.

Following out our allegory of a drama, we will now ask our readers to take one parting glance at the stage before a complete transformation takes place. In the opening scene, the curtain rose on a trackless wilderness, where savage hosts contended and grizzly death held sway.

In the closing scene we find the elements of discord removed, an established community enjoying the blessings of peace and commerce, while the African City itself has taken shape and form, and stands a solid centrepiece, engirt by smiling homes.

Hark! What sound is that, which falls upon the ear? Is it the menacing war chant of a Zulu host, or the deep roar of a prowling lion? Is it the dreadful crash of musketry, or the wail of sorrowing women? Thank God, no: those terrors have passed, and the music that closes the scene is the beating of the hammer on the anvil, and the lowing of the cattle in the fields.

So drops the curtain on the pregnant past; so fades away the scene, but not its memories.

CHAPTER VIII.

Sir George Grey.—The Royal Charter.—Opening of the First Parliament.—Maritzburg declared the Capital of the Colony.

IT is with very different feelings that we watch the rising of the curtain on the next act of our historical drama.

The same blazing sun that looked upon the stage as a wilderness illuminates it now, and reveals in the centre the figure of a British statesman.

Sir George Grey, then Governor of the Cape, had come to Maritzburg, by order of the Home Government, to enquire into the desirability of granting local representative government to the Colony, the European inhabitants of which now numbered eight thousand.

The prospects are hopeful, for on the distant mountains, with which we are so familiar, can be seen the thriving homesteads of the farmers. The cattle on a thousand hills are grazing peacefully, and men ride from point to point unarmed, while away off to the eastward, under the placid rule of Umpanda, the Zulus till the soil and, for the time being, neglect the spear.

Further still to the northward, over the Vaal, the malcontent Boers are enjoying their Elysian fields with never a

Briton near them, to their intense content and happiness, and the searching eyes of the statesman recognises in the present the promise of a happy future.

In the year 1856 a Royal Charter was granted, and on the 24th March, 1857, the curtain rises on another epoch scene.

A low, unpretentious building at the corner of Longmarket and Chapel Streets forms the centre of an eager throng.

The citizens are *en fete*, for at noon His Excellency the Lieutenant-Governor is about, in the name of Her Most Gracious Majesty Queen Victoria, to open the first Legislative Council in Natal. Maritzburg is aflame with bunting. As the hour approaches, guards of honour appear, His Excellency performs his function, and Natal becomes a State, while Maritzburg assumes new dignity, and for the first time can claim by right the title of a capital City.

SEA COAST OF NATAL.

THE RISE AND PROGRESS OF THE CITY.
CHAPTER IX.

A Bird's-eye View of the City.—Altitudes.—Scenery.—Contrasts.—Fort Napier.—Latitude.—Longtitude.—The Railway Station.

IN the first part of this volume we have endeavoured to record, as vividly as possible, such of the events of the past as were intimately associated with the founding of Maritzburg.

In this present part it will be our task to deal with the City as it is in its various aspects—as a place of residence, a commercial and educational centre, and, above all, as the capital of a Colony which has been truly described as one of Great Britain's strongholds in South Africa. In order to do this effectively, it is necessary first to present a general bird's-eye view of the City, and after dealing with its municipal history, then proceed to the description in detail of its various institutions.

The journey by rail from Durban to Maritzburg, which generally occupies a period of about four hours, lies through a panorama of scenery which is as varied as it is beautiful.

After leaving the sea level with its sub-tropical foliage, the line of railway traverses, on a gradually ascending scale, an open, agricultural district, rising in altitude above the sea to 3,000 feet, and falling as Maritzburg is approached, in latitude 29° 35" and longitude 30° 23", to 2,218 feet.

After leaving Fox Hill Station, which is about 2,810 feet above the sea, the road passes through cultivated lands.

H.R.H. PRINCE ALFRED LAYING FOUNDATION STONE MARITZBURG TOWN HALL.

Far away to the right, Table Mountain towers like a giant over its rugged and beautiful realm of forest and krantz. Slightly to the eastward, the district of Thornville can be seen. The line then sensibly falls, and a distinct difference is perceptible in the temperature as the train skirts the broad valley of Slang Spruit. Dotted here and there over a wide expanse of country small farms are to be seen, and the traveller who passes over the route for the first time will have considerable difficulty, in view of the evidences of permanent progress about him, in realising that the events dealt with in the earlier chapters of this work were really enacted so few years ago.

As the train sweeps on and the City itself comes in view, this feeling will be accentuated.

THE TOWN HALL.

Nestling under the noble Zwaartkop range of mountains lies Maritzburg, with its long stretches of tree-bordered streets, the ruddy tower of the Town Hall* looming out clear against the background of forest, while here, there, and everywhere the red-tiled roofs or the white walls of buildings gleam through the trees, and serve to beautify a picture well worthy of the brush of the artist.

---

*Since the above was penned a disastrous fire, resulting in the entire destruction of the stately edifice above depicted, occurred on the 12th July, 1898. The work of restoration is, however, now in progress.

Old colonists who reside in this neighbourhood are fond of telling how, but 30 years ago, this district was the haunt of the prowling leopard or the treacherous serpent.

Not one single trace of cultivation was visible, and the bright sunlight fell on nought but the productions of Nature in her wildest moods. Now we have the stately villa bowered in trees of a hundred varieties.

INTERIOR OF LATE TOWN HALL.

Owing to the enterprise of such men as Mr. Robert Topham, the wilderness in this locality has been transformed beyond belief, and the fact that the climate of Maritzburg is suitable for the production of timber trees is proved beyond all doubt.

In conversation with him and others, we learned that as far as possible, Australian trees should have the pre-terence, as the risk of fire to pines and conifers generally is great.

Most Australian trees have the double advantage of standing against fire and retuning freely from the stumps.

After the train has passed the Umsindusi bridge, the proximity of the City is evidenced on every hand. To the left, the slopes on which Fort Napier is built cut off the view; to the right, the Maritzburg College, in its wide and

RAILWAY STATION.

well-kept Park, is passed; while ahead to the westward and overshadowing the City, the Zwaartkop, or Black Mountain, bounds the view.

It is black only in name, however, for its slopes, during the summer months, at any rate, are bright with the varied tints of the rainbow, toned and softened by a delicate emerald mantle.

At intervals, deep kloofs and valleys are visible. Some of these constitute fashionable holiday resorts, and are also used as nurseries by the florists and gardeners of the City.

Further up, under the slopes of the mountains, and deep buried in the verdure of the forests, are romantic cascades and glades, whose existence would never be suspected by a casual observer.

INTERIOR OF RAILWAY STATION.

Returning to the line, as it approaches the City we find signs of advancement still increasing; to the left Fort Napier comes full in view, with the Union Jack crowning its summit. After one or two glimpses down the long, placid streets, the train steams under the groined roof of the finest completed railway station in Natal. The Station is situated at the top of Church Street, and is constructed of brick, with stone facings. The booking hall is 50 feet by 34, and has conveniently-placed booking and telegraph offices, constructed in highly finished woodwork.

Standing at the main exit of the Station overlooking the town, a view down the length of Church Street is

CHURCH STREET.

obtained. As many of the buildings in the immediate vicinity of the Station, date from the earliest days of Maritzburg, they do not strike the eye pleasingly, but further down the street, in the business portion of the City, there are numerous fine and lofty structures.

To the right of the street, and close to the Station, Government House is located.

CHAPTER X.

Municipal History.—The first Journals.—The first Town Board.—The Borough Endowment.—The Borough Seal.—Parks.—Schools.—Rash Speculation.—Trade Depression.—Effect of the Discovery of Diamonds.

THE original designers of the City were not hampered for want of space, and the result is that Maritzburg might be described as a town of magnificent distances.

In the earlier stages of its history this was undoubtedly a serious drawback, for, with the limited funds at the dis-

CHURCH STREET.

posal of the Corporation, it was impossible to apply anything like an adequate scheme for either hardening or lighting the streets.

The result of this was that for many years the place laboured under an evil reputation, not for crime, for that was almost unknown, but for inconvenience, and it became almost a fashionable thing, both for the local Press and the people, to level complaints of a more or less unjustifiable character at those who were public spirited enough to undertake the oftentimes thankless office of Town Councillor.

By degrees the straggling Dorp began to assume shape, and the long open spaces of veldt, in which the streets became lost, were built up or fenced off yard by yard, pavements were made, and the magnificent distances alluded to

LEGISLATIVE ASSEMBLY BUILDINGS.

were found to be none too wide for the requirements of the rising town.

At first, trade appeared to centre around the upper part of Longmarket and Chapel Streets, where the old Legislative Buildings were located, but by some mysterious process the route was altered, and Church Street became the principal thoroughfare.

In previous chapters we have already shown how the City was founded, and how, on the 15th of February, 1839, the first document dealing with regulations and instructions for fixing the situation and promoting the regularity of the town was promulgated, and further, how in 1843 the district of Natal was proclaimed a British Colony, in 1845 a province of the Cape Colony, and in 1856 a distinct Colony with an elective Legislature.

INTERIOR OF LEGISLATIVE ASSEMBLY.

In 1844 a weekly Dutch paper, called the *Natalier*, was started on anti-British lines. It was succeeded after a brief existence by the *Patriot*, which in turn gave place, in 1846, to the present *Natal Witness*. The first publisher and editor was Mr. David Dale Buchanan, an energetic and able journalist, and subsequently the first Mayor of Maritzburg. It was also to this gentleman's enterprise that the City was indebted for its first regular postal service to the seaport.

In 1847 a law was passed by the Cape Legislature for the creation of Municipal Boards in the towns and villages of Natal, and in 1848 a meeting of resident householders was held for the purpose of taking advantage of the provisions of this law, and of passing the necessary municipal regulations. The municipality was divided into wards The governing municipal body consisted of a Board of Commis-

CHURCH STREET.

sioners, composed of five members, and invested with similar powers to the present Town Council.

The first Board elected consisted of Mr. A. T. Caldecott, (Chairman), and Messrs. William Van Aardt, Philip Ferreira, Dr. B. Poortman, and P. J. Jung.

The first meeting held by the Commissioners was on the 27th March, 1848, when sundry officers were appointed, among others, Mr. John Polydore Steele as Town Clerk,

Market Master, Town Collector, and Overseer of Waterworks, at a salary of £100 per annum.

One of the members of the Board, Mr. P. Ferreira, afterwards Mayor of Maritzburg, was appointed Treasurer, and held the office for a number of years, the remuneration attached to it being a " vote of thanks."

Public meetings were called for the purpose of levying rates when occasion required.

The newly-formed Borough was endowed with 26,000 acres of town lands, and all unalienated erven within the City.

MOUNTED POLICE BARRACKS.

To support its dignity a Borough seal was necessary, and one, designed by a Mr. Saunderson, was adopted.

It consists of five stars surmounted by an elephant, with the word " Umgungunhlovo," the Kafir name for the City, underneath.

The literal signification of the word is " The conqueror of the Elephant," and was originally applied to Dingaan and his kraal.

By a natural transition it came to signify the seat of Government and Capital of the Colony. The centre star refers to the star of Bethlehem, in allusion to the discovery of Natal on Christmas Day, while the other four represent the southern cross, an emblem of Christianity, and indicative of the Colony's geographical position.

The gradual increase in the municipal revenue consequent on the steady growth of the town soon enabled the Corporation to undertake comparatively large public works. Bridges were built across the Umsindusi River, improvements were effected in the main thoroughfares, and tree-

PARK FOOT BRIDGE.

planting, to which the City owes so much of its beauty, began to engage considerable attention.

Numerous blocks of town lands lots were acquired by settlers at prices ranging from £2 10s. to £5 per acre, while other lots were let out for agricultural and brickmaking purposes. With a foresight which cannot be too highly commended, the Corporation determined that before the Borough lands were extensively taken up by purchase or lease they would benefit by the bitter experience of large British cities, and, ere it was too late, preserve open spaces or recreation grounds for the public.

Those three veteran colonists and citizens whose names are household words, to wit, Sir John Akerman, K C.M.G., Mr. W. E. Bale, J.P., and the late Mr. Wm. Leathern, were the first to move in this direction, and one of the

COMMERCIAL ROAD.

results of their action is the Alexandra Park. The finances of the Council were not equal at that time to any heavy expenditure in connection with the beautifying of that now popular place of resort, but the site was reserved (in extent 162 acres), and in 1863 secured by deed of trust as a public park. Subsequent Councils vied with each other in increasing its attractions, and have followed the good example of their far-seeing predecessors by reserving sites for parks in other parts of the Borough, where they may be of inestimable value to future generations.

Considerably over £3,000 has recently been spent, still further improving the Alexandra Park, which is now well worthy to rank with any in South Africa. Northern Park, on the road to Town Bush Valley, has an area of 20 acres, and Albany Park, so named in honour of His Grace the late Duke of Albany, has an area of 57 acres, and is situated near the Zwaartkop Railway Station.

In 1861 the Town Council liberally responded to a proposition made by Governor Scott for the establishment of a College or High School, and its endowment jointly by the Government and Corporation. The Government provided £6,000, and the Corporation, £5,000, together with a site for the College. The old High School Building, now converted into a Boys' Model School, was erected with the funds thus provided. In a subsequent chapter, the College and other Educational Institutions will be fully dealt with.

During the years 1864 and 1867 the City passed through a period of great commercial depression. The The rivalry of banks and other fiinancial institutions offered unusual facilities for borrowing money. This had the effect of stimulating enterprise to an unwholesome degree, and much capital was sunk in unproductive ventures. The high rents levied for the use of dwellings induced many to borrow money for the purpose of erecting their own houses, in order to escape the exactions of landlords; dwellings being thus increased beyond the requirements of the town. The income derivable from rents was considerably curtailed, and the inevitable result of over speculation in other directions began to be apparent.

The complaisancy of the banks and their readiness to make advances came to a speedy conclusion, and then it

CHURCH STREET.

would appear that they erred as grievously in the opposite
direction, for in order to secure themselves against loss, they
exercised the utmost severity towards their debtors. Several
firms had made extensive use of accommodation bills, while
the customary mode of paying for goods was by means of

EDENDALE FALLS.

promissory notes which were renewed from time to time, and
passed from hand to hand, until they came to be regarded
almost as a paper currency.

The reckless manner in which persons endorsed bills,
and the utter absence of care in financial transactions, could

only produce one result. A large firm transacting business in every part of the Colony failed with £100,000 liabilities, and inflicted many losses, principally on the farming community. This was followed by another failure with £50,000 liabilities, and as everyone had been so ready to oblige his neighbour by endorsing bills for him, few people knew to what extent they were involved. When the banks began to exercise pressure many sought refuge in the Insolvency Court, and the inability of those to meet their liabilities involved others in their fall. In the City the depression was perhaps more felt than in other parts of the Colony, for the absence of trade compelled many mercantile houses to discharge numbers of their employés.

NATIVE CONSTABLE.

The Corporation found it impossible to collect more than a third of its revenue, and was compelled to have an over-draft at the bank of £10,000 —more than two years' revenue at that time. The discovery of the Diamond Fields in 1870 came as a god-send to the City, for the new industries attracted large numbers of Colonists and citizens to Kimberley, where many of them were successful in acquiring wealth. On their return to Natal they bought back the properties, in many instances, which they had been forced to abandon during the financial crisis, while others again invested their money in houses and farms. The impetus thus given to trade enabled the City to recover from the commercial depression and the increased wealth of individuals reacted beneficially on the whole community.

CHAPTER XI.

Preparations for the Zulu War.—Maritzburg Fortified.—The Boer War.—Trade Depression.—Effect of Gold Discoveries.—Excitement—Wild Speculation.—Financial Disasters—Recovery.—Steady Progress.

ZULU WAR MONUMENT.

THE preparations for the Zulu War in 1878, the calling out of the mounted volunteers, the organising and equipment of corps of irregular cavalry and Native contingents, the constant arrival of troops from Home and their departure to the Zulu country, occasioned great stir in Maritzburg, which was the base of supplies during the campaign.

The dreadful news of the battle of Isandhlwana not only brought grief and desolation to many Colonist's homes, but led the citizens to realise how imminent was the danger of a Zulu invasion. The City Guard which had been formed received large accessions to its numbers, the burgesses showing a ready and willing spirit to take their full part in the defence of the City. Sentries were posted nightly throughout the streets, and the challenge was constantly heard. One large laager was constructed at the Post Office, embracing that part of the City lying between Commercial Road, Timber Street, Pietermaritz Street and Longmarket Street. Two others were also erected at the Gaol and the Camp respectively. The streets and shops were barricaded and loop-holed, and every preparation made to give the Zulus a warm reception should they come. The defences were provisioned, and three guns fired from Fort Napier was to be the signal for the inhabitants to get into laager. Vague rumours got about that the Zulus were

THE SHEPSTONE MEMORIAL.

close to the City, and the people were in a state of suspense, not knowing what an hour might bring forth. The news of the gallant defence of Rorke's Drift, by which the Colony was doubtless saved from invasion, relieved the spell of intense excitement, and the citizens began to breathe more freely. The subsequent events of the war lie beyond the scope of these pages, but reference must be made to the death of the Prince Imperial of France, the reception of whose body was perhaps one of the most mournful and impressive pageants that the City has ever witnessed. Many in Maritzburg had experienced the same loss that his mother, the widowed Empress, was deploring, and memories

POST OFFICE.

of Isandhlwana gave point to the grief and heartfelt sympathy everywhere expressed.

Close following on hostilities in Zululand came the trouble in the Transvaal, and the City once more was astir with the movements of troops.

Although the British-Boer War was in no sense a Colonists' quarrel, the proximity of the scene of hostilities caused great interest to be taken in the struggle, and the news of the battles of Laing's Nek and Amajuba stirred the City to its depths.

Scarcely was this war over than another period of commercial depression set in, and for some years local trade was in a very bad way indeed.

Again the unexpected happened, as in the case of the Diamond Fields, for in 1886 the discovery of gold deposits at Moodie's and Barberton revived languishing enterprise.

ST. PETER'S BELLS.

The formation of syndicates appeared to become the aim of everyone's existence and numerous representatives were sent to "peg out" claims on the new "El Dorado."

Companies were floated in the City for the working of these properties, and considerable sums of money were fruitlessly spent through the inexperience alike of promoters and prospectors.

The gold fever appeared to have smitten everyone, and the talk of the town for some months was of nothing save reefs, leaders, lodes, assays, and shares.

Again trouble dawned, for over-speculation bore its inevitable fruits, and many of those who had invested their little all were unable to hold on, and so perforce had to succumb to the pressure of circumstances.

RT. REVD. J. W. COLENSO, D.D.,
LATE BISHOP OF NATAL.

As a sort of miracle the discovery of the Witwatersrand Goldfields took place at this time, and like the passing of a meteor re-illuminated the darkening prospects of the City. Practically speaking the new rush to the high veld of the Transvaal was led by Maritzburgers.

A camp was established near where Jeppestown is now located, and called " Natal'Spruit Camp."

Many City representatives or syndicates secured valuable properties, which have since, as all the world knows, maintained their high standard.

The attention of the London Stock Exchange was directed to the South African Goldfields, shares in the leading companies rose to enormous prices, and many tottering firms in the City not only recovered their balance, but became transformed into wealthy and influential institutions.

It was not all *coleur de rose*, however. Again over-speculation brought forth its fruits of depression, but this time in

BAND STAND.

a less marked degree. A steady recovery soon took place, and the industry settled itself on regularly established and remunerative lines.

The effect on the City was important, as several of the leading companies have their head offices in it, and are investing their profits in the erection of well-appointed offices and buildings.

Sixteen years ago Maritzburg was the terminus of the Natal Government Railways, and it was confidently predicted by many that when the line was extended further north, the Capital City of Natal would sink into an insignificant village, inhabited by a few officials, and would become inert and defunct as far as commerce and social progress were concerned.

True it is that the forwarding agent and the transport-rider have gone elsewhere to ply their callings, still Maritz-

RIVER SCENE.

burg has steadily progressed in every desirable direction. Its population has increased within ten years by 75 per cent. The agricultural districts, of which it is the centre, have greatly improved, and its farmers are daily awakening to the necessity of a closer and more scientific system of agriculture.

Despite the ravages of locusts, drought, and rinderpest, which have unusually affected the Colony, they are, as a class, fairly prosperous, and as a natural result the merchants and traders of the city share their prosperity.

As will be shown in the chapter on Municipal finances, large sums of money have been spent on surface drainage and the construction of roads and bridges. The effective maintenance of about 45 miles of streets, of a width ranging from 60 to 80 feet, besides suburban roads in a country where heavy rain-storms are frequent, necessarily involves constant expenditure, which could not have been provided had the revenues of the City been as unsatisfactory as certain ill-informed persons at one time attempted to maintain through the public Press. A well-managed Police Force, composed of 25 Europeans and 40 Native constables, is maintained, and law and order are upheld as rigidly as in any old-established British Borough.

The system of water supply established by the original Dutch settlers was that of open watercourses called "sluits," by means of which the supply was led through the streets.

The water was thus either available for motive power, irrigation, or domestic use, and the oxygenating properties of running water kept the supply pure and wholesome. As the town became more thickly populated, there arose a greater need for the thorough supervision of these watercourses, and for definition of the rights of householders to the use of the water.

At first the Municipal authorities shrank from undertaking an extensive scheme of water supply by pipes, and in 1875 the Municipality expressed a hope that some company might be induced to take the matter up. Fortunately for the Borough no company came forward, and the Corporation had at last to deal with the question, which was becoming more urgent every day. Finally plans and specifications were called for in 1878, and a premium was offered for the best. Messrs. Beardmore, Barnes and Twigg, an

English firm of Engineers, were the successful competitors, they undertaking to have the work carried out according to specifications at a cost of about £30,000. In 1881 the Waterworks were formally opened. Extensions of the original plan have since brought up the cost to nearly £60,000, but the excellent quality of the water is a priceless advantage.

A considerable revenue is now being derived by the City from its use for other than domestic purposes. The utmost care is taken to ensure purity by a systematic supervision of the sources of supply and periodical cleansing of the reservoirs and filteration beds.

It is to this care that the people of the City are indebted for the marvellous immunity from serious sickness which is enjoyed.

CHAPTER XII.

BOROUGH FINANCES.

IT has been said that the key-note of modern social legislation is its trust in local authorities, and the burden of duties imposed by statute on those authorities has so steadily grown that at the present day their control is felt in almost every department of life. In Natal, the public policy in its relation to Municipal Corporations and other urban local bodies has been a liberal one. The fullest authority is conferred upon them to maintain good rule and government within their respective boundaries, and when new circumstances arise which require special provision to meet them, fresh powers are given in no grudging spirit.

While on the one hand large powers are conferred, and duties thereby imposed, the means needful for the effectual exercise of these powers, and the discharge of the relative duties, are not withheld. To every Municipal Corporation and Local Board in the Colony, soon after their creation, the Government has transferred in freehold all lands which had not previously been alienated within the limits of their various jurisdictions. In each case these lands comprise several thousands of acres, and constitute a splendid endowment for the newly-created Borough or Township. In addition to this, rating powers are given over the freehold value of all immovable property within their limits, and certain licenses, which in older countries pertain to the revenues of the Crown, here help to swell the local exchequer.

To the youthful town, hardly yet emerged from its rural state, the lands with which it has been endowed form a valuable commonage and grazing ground for the cattle and horses of its citizens The township grows in importance, its population increases, merchant princes arise who require country residences. then we hear of suburban villa sites, and the town awakes to find that its Town Lands can be put to a better use than grazing ground for its citizens' cattle.

On the establishment of the Municipality of Pietermaritzburg in 1854, the City was endowed with 26,000 acres of Town Lands and all the unalienated erven within the existing City. The revenues of the City for the first three or four years scarcely averaged £1,000 per annum. There was much to be done, and little to do it with. Promissory notes, guaranteed by individual members of Council, were no uncommon feature of the financial history. Bridges were wanted for the rivers, otherwise impassable in the wet season, roads had to be constructed, and the other demands of the small body of taxpayers satisfied in some way or other. For relief the worried Councillors turned to the Town Lands, and a number of lots were sold, and the proceeds applied to the construction of public works. The steady growth of the town, and the consequent increase of the Municipal revenues, soon brought about a sounder policy. Application was made to the Legislature for borrowing powers, and in 1864 and 1866 Bills were passed enabling the Council to raise funds by the issue of debentures, secured by the revenue of the Borough and the unsold Town Lands. The credit of the City was, however, so little esteemed in those days that *nine per cent.* was the rate of interest the Council had to pay. Some of the debentures were issued for a period of fifty years, and are not a pleasant subject of reflection to those who have now to deal with the finances of the Borough, whatever they may be to the fortunate holders of the stock. The borrowing powers thus obtained were not exhausted until 1880, by which time the rate of interest which had to be paid was six per cent To provide for the redemption of this loan on maturity, a sinking fund was established, into which the proceeds of sales of Town Lands between the years 1964 and 1880 were paid The portion of the loan still to be redeemed amounts to £24,800, and the sinking fund by means of which it is to be redeemed to £24,750, a sum nearly equal in amount to the loan itself.

In 1882 further borrowing powers to the extent of £100,000 were obtained, and the money raised by debentures, bearing interest at six per cent. This loan was principally spent in the construction of waterworks, the erection of a new Market Hall and Police Station, and the macadamising of the principal streets of the City. The redemption of the previous loan having been provided for by means of its relative sinking fund, the proceeds of town lands sales were made available for the establishment of a second sinking fund to meet the debentures of Loan No. 2 on their falling due. The outstanding debt in respect of this second loan at present amounts to £64,500, while the sinking fund, which is yearly increasing, amounts to £8,400.

In 1888 a law was passed to enable the Municipality to consolidate the existing loans, and to borrow up to the limit previously authorised, namely, £150,000. Power was given to issue inscribed stock, and to convert the two loans before referred to into this class of security. Unfortunately for the Town Council, the debenture-holders are too well aware of the value of their holdings, and are quite pleased to keep what they have, failing to see any advantage to them in conversion. The Council has thus, for the most part, been compelled to wait until the debentures have become due before they could take advantage of the provisions of the law of 1888 with respect to consolidation. The amount of stock issued under the operation of this law at present amounts to £49,200. This bears interest at five per cent., and was readily taken up in the Colony at an average premium of seven per cent. The Consolidated Stock Law further enabled the Council to release portions of the sinking funds, in proportion to the amount of the debentures which were retired and converted into Consolidated Stock, and with the moneys thus released the larger portion of the cost of the erection of the former Town Hall was defrayed. It was, however, found necessary to raise a short-dated loan of fifteen years, in amount £15,000, to pay the balance of the cost, and to carry out certain urgent works in connection with road macadamising. This loan bears interest at five per cent., and was raised with the consent of His Excellency the Governor under the provisions of the Municipal Corporations Law of the Colony.

The growing importance of the City, and the pressing demands for a better water supply, a complete system of surface drainage, the claims of suburban residents for better roads, and the necessity for establishing a better system of electric lighting, led the Council in 1896 to determine that for the future the cost of all permanent works should be paid for out of loan funds. With this object in view, an Act was passed in 1896 empowering the Corporation to raise a sum of £100,000 for the carrying out of permanent public works. The stock to be issued was to be Consolidated Stock, as defined in the Consolidated Loan Law of 1888, and the rate of interest was not to exceed four per cent. Tenders were invited for £50,000 of stock (being for £40,000 of this loan, and £10,000 for debentures retired under the operations of the law of 1888), and it was issued at three per cent., realising an average of 98 per £100 worth of stock.

The importance of the City could not be better shown than by contrasting the rate of interest payable in 1866, viz., nine per cent., with the loan rate of three per cent. which is now paid. The borrowing powers obtained in 1896 have been found insufficient to do all that the Council wishes in the way of the betterment of the City, and subsequent legislation has given further powers to the extent of £150,000. A large portion of this will be spent on electric lighting plant, and the revenue from this industrial undertaking is estimated not only to provide for the working expenses, but also to meet charges for interest on the capital expenditure and depreciation of the plant.

The following table shows the existing loans of the City of Pietermaritzburg, rate of interest payable thereon, and due date of each :—

Return showing Loans raised by Corporation of Maritzburg, due date, and rate of interest thereon.

Year Due.	Loan No. 1.	Loan No. 2. (Consol. Stock).	Loan No. 3	Loan No. 4.	Rate of Interest.
1899	...	2,000	...	...	6 per cent.
1900	100	...	...	...	5½ ,,
...	2,400	...	...	...	6 ,
1902	...	11,800	...	...	6
1903	...	5,800	...	...	6

Year Due.	Loan No. 1.	Loan No. 2. (Consol Stock.)	Loan No. 3.	Loan No. 4.	Rate of Interest.
1904	...	6,500	...	...	6 per cent.
...	1,000	...	...	...	9 ,,
1905	200	...	...	...	9 ,,
1906	13,500	...	...	...	9 ,,
1907	4,900	12,400	...	...	6 ,,
...	300	...	...	...	9 ,,
1908	2,400	...	...	...	9 ,,
...	...	4,500	...	...	6 ,,
1909	...	...	...	15,000	5 ,,
...	...	8,900	...	...	6 ,,
1912	...	500	...	...	6 ,,
1913	...	800	...	...	6 ,,
1914	...	200	...	...	6 ,,
1931	...	2,800	...	...	6 ,,
1932	...	7,300	...	...	6 ,,
1939	...	...	49,200	...	5 ,,
...	...	...	50,000	...	3 ,,
Total	24,800	63,500	99,200	15,000	
Original Issue	50,000	100,000	..	15,000	

The principal sources of the Municipal revenue are rates, licenses, market dues, water charges, and rents.

The following is an approximate summary of the revenue at the present time :—

Rates	£22,500
Licenses	4,750
Market Dues	2,700
Water Charges	3,000
Rents	2,500
Other Sources	2,050
	£37,500

In addition to the foregoing there is also the revenue derived from electric light supplied, interest on sinking fund securities, and proceeds of land sales, which bring up the gross revenue to nearly £45,000.

The following table, showing the Municipal revenue since the year of incorporation, will be instructive as illustrating the gradual and steady growth of the Borough :—

1891-2	...	...	...	£30,907
1892-3	...	...	...	35,587
1893-4	...	...	...	34,577
1894-5	...	...	...	37,156
1895-6	...	...	...	39,760
1896-7	...	...	...	44,583

In 1871 the value of rateable property within the Borough was £270,261. In 1881 this had increased to £1,052,013. In 1891 it was £1,327,000, and this year it is £2,252,570.

Government property, churches, schools, and charitable institutions are exempt from rates, and the value of these premises within the Borough is estimated at £870,000.

The chief assets of the Municipality include freehold land and buildings to the value of nearly £300,000, and waterworks, which have cost £70,000. Among the buildings may be mentioned the Town Hall, Telegraph Offices, Market Hall, and three Police Stations, most of which will be been described in other portions of this work.

CHAPTER XIII.

PUBLIC BUILDINGS.

IF the number and size of public buildings be regarded as a test of a town's relative importance, the claims of Maritzburg to be counted among the most prominent cities in South Africa rest upon very substantial grounds.

The past decade has witnessed the demolition of many primitive structures, originally used for public purposes, and the erection of stately and commodious edifices, calculated to meet the increasing demands of a progressive community.

Whatever may be the failings of the colonists of Natal, or the citizens of Maritzburg, they cannot by any means be accused of want of confidence in the future of their country.

The public buildings in the City are of two classes, one belonging to the Government of the Colony, the other being the property of the Municipality. Of the former, Government House, the residence of the Governor of the Colony, is a solidly-built mansion, which has recently been enlarged. The Supreme Court and the premises of the General Post are, with other Government Departments, accommodated in a large building facing the Town Hall. The Legislative Assembly building is probably one of the finest structures in the City, being well finished and elaborately furnished with Colonial made furniture. The Colonial Offices, now in course of erection in Church Street, when completed will constitute an imposing and beautiful addition to the street frontage. In extent and convenience the building will be in every respect worthy of the progressive nature of the Colony.

In the suburbs, extensive barracks for the Natal Police have been erected.

The Natal Government Lunatic Asylum, besides having one of the best Town Lands sites, is a very fine cluster of buildings, standing in their own grounds.

In addition to minor Government institutions there are three large schools, one for boys and two for girls, all of which are good modern structures, specially designed for the purpose for which they are used.

Grey's Hospital, which receives a Government grant of £2,200 per annum, is also a commodious structure, occupying a site of eight acres, and is endowed with a grant of 1,000 acres from the Corporation.

The Municipal buildings comprise a well-designed Market Hall, erected at a cost of £8,000.

The new Borough Police Station, costing £7,000, has taken the place of the old historic structure which served the double purpose of station and gaol. In close proximity to this, the new Town Hall stands, occupying a corner of Church Street and Commercial Road. From the very earliest days of the Corporation a building of this class had been talked about, but the idea was opposed by many leading Colonists, who forwarded a petition to the Corporation in which they stated that such a building was unnecessary. The event has proved how utterly mistaken these persons were. In 1860, when H.R.H. the Duke of Edinburgh visited Maritzburg, he performed the function of laying the foundation stone. Great rejoicings and festivities celebrated the event, but the stone lay for thirty years a silent witness of the small income of the City.

In 1888, Mr. J. J. Chapman, then Mayor, laid before the Town Council a scheme for the consolidation of the existing debt of the Municipality, its conversion into inscribed stock, issued at a low rate of interest, the gradual release of the sinking funds, and their expenditure on permanent public works.

By this scheme the Council was in a position to undertake the erection of a Town Hall, and in order to make the building as large as possible, and suited for the future needs of the Borough, application was made to the Government for its co-operation. This being accorded, the Council adopted the proposal.

Under the arrangements made, the Government became tenants of a portion of the building for a number of years.

The following is a description of the Hall :— The style is free Renaissance, and as this has had as it were a new birth in Britain, grown up from modern needs, it can only be described as "Victorian," with piazza and balconies, designed to especially suit the scorching suns of Natal.

As to the internal arrangements, the rooms are all large, airy, and well lighted.

The Main Hall is a noble room, and well proportioned, being 114 feet long, including the proscenium, by 53 feet wide.

The Council Chamber, 45½ feet by 27½ feet, is also a fine room, and has an open balcony running along the entire front. This is approached by broad French casements.

The Main Entrance Hall in Church Street is 18 feet by 16 feet, with an antecedent vestibule.

The Entrance Hall in Commercial Road, 28 feet by 24 feet, is larger, and contains a grand staircase

There is also an annexe to this Hall, 12 feet by 8 feet, and an antecedent vestibule. Cloak-rooms are attached to both entrances.

The Municipal Government Rooms to the north side of Commercial Road, having a frontage to Church Street, are ample in space and convenience. There is also a subsidiary staircase and entrance at the north-east corner.

The Town Clerk and Staff and Borough Engineer are amply provided for ; the Council Chamber, already mentioned, retiring rooms for members of the Council, Mayor's Parlour and appurtenances, all being richly furnished. The Legislative Council, or Upper House, occupies some chambers overlooking the Church Street entrance.

The south-west side of Commercial Road, and south semi-front, are all occupied by Government officials. The Resident Magistrate's Court, 40 feet by 22 feet, is situated here. There are three rooms for the Magistrate and staff, for two Indian and Native interpreters, another for constables and witnesses, and two for prisoners of both sexes.

On the first floor of this portion, the Audit Department has five large rooms, and extensive basement accommodation below the Magistrate's Court.

The Mining and Agricultural Department occupy the rest of the corridor.

In the rear of the basement are Kitchen, Store, and Retiring Rooms, while underneath the Main Hall vast Cellerage has been constructed. The entire building is lighted by electricity.

A magnificent organ, erected mainly by subscription of burgesses and others, at the cost of about £4,000, has been placed in the main hall.

The tower, which is about 120 feet in height, contains a large clock and chimes of bells.

The building was opened on the 15th June, 1893, and the total cost was £42,317.

Of churches and chapels there are many in the City, the most notable perhaps being the Cathedrals of St. Saviour's and St. Peter's. Every other denomination is strongly represented, and the style of building, together with their interior fittings, are sufficient evidence of the religious vitality of the City. It may be interesting to mention here that the remains of that world-famed prelate, the Right Reverend J. W. Colenso, D.D., formerly Lord Bishop of Natal, repose beside the altar of St. Peter's Cathedral.

Of monuments, Maritzburg possesses four, artistically and elaborately-finished specimens.

Opposite the Town Hall, at the corner of Church Street and Commercial Road, a magnificent cluster of white marble figures has been placed to commemorate the names of those who fell in the Zulu War.

In the front of the General Post Office a column has been erected in honour of those Volunteers who died in the suppression of the Langalibalele rebellion.

In front of the Legislative Buildings there is a white marble statue of Her Majesty the Queen.

In the Court Gardens, a monument surmounted by a life-sized figure of Sir Theophilus Shepstone is placed.

In the vestibule of the Town Hall, a marble bust of Sir Bartle Frere fittingly recalls the name and life of one of the best and noblest Governors South Africa has ever seen.

ST. SAVIOUR'S CHURCH.

In the vestibule of the Maritzburg College and in various Churches, numerous tablets in marble and brass testify to the valour and worth of past leaders, warriors, and pioneers, whose names and lives were associated with the City and its history.

The very handsome Maritzburg College, which will be dealt with later on, occupies a commanding site on the south-western slope of the beautiful Alexandra Park.

The Story of an African City. 79

One of the most important advances recently made by the City is the extensive provision made for the supply of electric light. The Electric Power Station building has been designed on the lines of the electric lighting stations in the large towns at Home, and seems well calculated to ensure efficiency of working. The station contains a spacious boiler house, engine-room, pump-room, workshop, and an office and testing-room combined. In the boiler-room pro-

THE UNVEILING OF THE QUEEN'S STATUE.

vision is made for eight boilers, laid in pairs, of 85 nominal horse power each, easy steaming. In the engine-room will be six engines and dynamos direct coupled, each capable of supplying the power for 1,000 lamps of 16-candle power each. In connection with each dynamo a concrete pit has been built so that the heavy field magnets will swing partly under ground, which obviates the necessity of the dynamos being erected at an inconvenient height above ground The cost of the station and plant when complete will be about

£17,000, and the total cost of the whole installation, which includes the work throughout the town, about £32,650. The underground cables throughout the City are now being laid.

The Diamond Jubilee Pavilion, the foundation stone of which was laid on the 22nd of June last, has been erected to commemorate the sixtieth year of the reign of Her Majesty the Queen.

It faces the Oval in the Alexandra Park, and is an imposing edifice, furnishing spacious accommodation both for the public and sportsmen. On the ground floor the central feature is a large Dining Hall, from either side of which corridors extend, giving access to suites of rooms for Committees, Clubs, Press, Scorers, Caterer, &c. Towards the front, opening on the proposed lawn, is an Entrance Hall and Dressing Rooms fitted up with lavatory facilities for the use of competing teams. Flanking the main structure are a Bar and Tea-room, while situated outside the reserved area are Refreshment Rooms accessible to the general public frequenting the Park. Extending over the main structure is a Grand Stand, containing accommodation for over 500 persons, and at either end covered pavilions, giving additional provision for spectators. Surmounting these pavilions are raised turrets of picturesque design. An excellent view is also obtained from the look-out on the top of the main roof. The contractor for the whole of the works, which cost over £4,000, has been Mr. E. Wheller, and the work has been carried out under the superintendence of Mr. William Lucas, architect, of this City, who is responsible for the design of the handsome structure.

We are indebted to Dr. Campbell Watt for the following notes on the Sanatorium, which is situated in the upper end of Loop Street on a site unrivalled in the City for healthiness and beauty of prospect. It is one of the latest additions to the public institutions, the foundation stone having been laid by Bishop Jolivet, O.M.I., on September 18th, 1897, and will prove a boon to the sick of the City and neighbourhood. The cost of the erection was £6,000, and the site £2,000. The management is in the hands of the Augustinian Sisterhood of the Mercy of Jesus. The Reverend Mother Superior and Sisters form the nursing staff, and are all nurses of high training and long experience.

The building faces the south, and embraces a magnificent view of the surrounding country. To the left lies the range of hills crowned by "Cope's Folly." All in front sweeps the gentle slope of the town lands, with Table Mountain rising grandly in the distance beyond, and the College, the Park, and the Umsinduzi River filling in the foreground. The occasional strains of martial music stealing up from the Park add an additional spell to the prospect; and prove grateful to the ears of the sufferers within. The building consists of three flats and attics, and has accommodation for over 30 patients. The wards are 20 in number, the majority being intended for the use of one patient only. In the ground floor there are the dining rooms, sitting room, two wards, bath room (with hot and cold water and shower), kitchen, and offices. There are seven wards on the first floor and two nurses' rooms. The second floor is all devoted to wards; while the attics form the bedrooms for the nurses. In the corridor of each flat is a washstand with hot and cold water. An elevator runs from basement to attic. The whole building is fitted with electric light, and electric bells are everywhere. Two wide balconies overlook the Park, and, with the corridors, form splendid promenades. All the furniture is of a high class, combining usefulness with elegance. The wards, particularly, are beautifully furnished with complete bedroom suites and appliances. Each ward possesses a fireplace, and fanlights are fitted above all doors and windows to assist the ventilators when necessary.

On an average the small wards measure 15 feet by 12 ; and the ceilings are lofty. All the walls in the building are painted, in order to secure perfect cleanliness. The ventilation and drainage are excellent.

The operating room stands apart from the main building, and is well lighted from the roof and sides.

The grounds attached to the Sanatorium will be laid out in a tasteful style with walks and garden houses.

One commendable feature of this well-equipped institution is that each patient selects his own medical attendant, there being no regular medical staff attached ; and clergymen of all denominations are at liberty to visit their sick. Convalescents may be admitted in the event of there being room to spare, the sick having the preference.

The charges have a wide range—from 5s. to 12s. 6d. per day ; while the poor are admitted at reduced rates, or free.

CHAPTER XIV.

Institutions and Industries.

THE Natal Society was established in 1851, and had for its objects the development of the physical, commercial, agricultural, and other resources of Natal and Eastern Africa.

The Library and Museum were established, lectures were delivered on various subjects connected with the objects of the Society, and a prize of £25 was given for an essay on the "Moral and physical condition of Natal, with practical suggestions as to its capabilities and means of supplying an industrial population."

Considerable interest was manifested in the work of the Society, numerous donations of books and money were made by its friends, and the Government assisted it with a small grant from the public funds. The limited resources of the Society, however, rendered it impracticable to do more than direct attention to the various important subjects it sought to deal with, and the Library Department was the only branch which seemed likely to prove ultimately useful. Recent events, however, have belied this supposition.

In 1872 the Society took advantage of the provisions of an Ordinance then passed to become a body corporate. The present Library was erected in 1878.

During recent years the Museum Department so largely increased as to render additional accommodation absolutely necessary.

The fine large hall, now again too small for its purpose, adjoining the Library, was constructed, and space secured for the valuable collection of curious and interesting specimens which continue to be sent to it from various parts of Africa and elsewhere.

The success of this department of the Natal Society's labours is largely due to the untiring efforts of Mr. Morton Green, J.P., who has in many other important ways rendered distinguished service to the Colony.

At present the Library contains about 13,000 volumes, and the circulation of books and magazines is about 36,000 per annum.

The Government makes a grant of £350 per annum to the Society, and the subscriptions amount to a little over £400.

The usefulness of the institution is fully shown by the attendance of readers, which is, on an average, 400 per diem.

Several building societies were established very early in the City's history, and met with considerable success. At the present time there are no fewer than four terminable and two permanent societies of this kind, with a capital of about

£100,000. In the progress of the town these institutions have played no mean part, and few cities of equal size can show so large a portion of dwellings whose occupiers are also their proprietors.

The encouragement of thrift and self-help amongst the working classes, who are the backbone of the community, are the primary objects of building societies, and the large measure of success they have achieved speaks well for the provident habits for this section of the population.

No less important feature in the welfare of the community is the large membership of friendly and benefit societies. The earliest established was a branch of the Oddfellows and the Lodge here is one of most prosperous in the whole Order, possessing funds to the extent of £6,000, and a membership of over 200. Courts of Foresters and Shepherds also flourish, and the most recent addition to the number of these institutions is a benefit society established among the coloured population, which has already made such progress as to possess a well-built hall for holding meetings.

The mystic letters emblazoned on the front of the City Young Men's Christian Association indicate that within is housed one of the 6,000 centres of work scattered throughout the globe, with a membership of half-a-million, drawn from 26 distinct nations, and speaking some 17 different languages.

Thirty-one years after the founding of the movement, and ten years after the establishment of the South African Association at Capetown, on the 26th March, 1875, a meeting was called to consider the formation of an Association in this City.

The enterprise that has recently so markedly characterised the movement has been its leading feature throughout its history. Among the earlier names on the roll of membership there are not a few who have proved themselves valued members of the civic and political life of South Africa.

Within five years of its inception a building site was secured, and shortly afterwards, on the 23rd of May, 1881, a Hall, accommodating 250 persons, and costing £1,600, was opened.

In 1882 a Boys' Institute was started, and in 1887, on the retirement of the first President, the Rev. John Smith,

Y.M.C.A. HALL.

M.A., the present Attorney-General, Hon. Henry Bale, Q.C., M.L.A., became President.

In 1893 a spacious Gymnasium was erected. By 1894 the work of the Association had grown so much, almost exclusively under the valued services of the honorary officers. that it was found necessary to engage a Secretary who would be prepared to devote his whole time to the consolidating of the existing efforts, and laying the foundations of new forms of usefulness. Mr. William Lucas, who had just arrived in the Colony, having had extensive experience in Y.M.C.A. matters, accepted the appointment of General Secretary for two years.

Through the support given to a most successful bazaar in 1895, the sum of nearly £800 was paid towards the liquidation of the debt on the Gymnasium, and shortly afterwards, through the liberality of a few friends, the balance of £400 was extinguished.

The City Association was well represented at the first South African Conference, held in Johannesburg at the close of 1895, when Mr. Bale, the President, was elected President of the Conference, and who, by-the-way, was re-elected at the second Conference held recently in Capetown.

A few years ago the President was also appointed a corresponding member of the English National Council of Y.M.C.A.'s, on the motion of Sir George Williams, the founder of the movement.

In March, 1896, the constitution was revised so as to admit any young man of moral character as an associate, associates having all the privileges of membership, save the right to residence on the premises and taking part in business meetings.

Among the advantages thus secured are home from-home influences, the formation of valued friendships, a healthful rallying ground, an impulse to generous endeavour, " a stimulus to follow life's upper, rather than its lower, pathways."

Through correspondence and exchange of literature with kindred associations throughout the world, the Assocation is moreover a veritable bureau of cosmopolitan information. The facilities for correspondence and introductions are therefore indispensible to progressive young men.

On Jubilee Day, 1897, the foundation-stone of extensive additions was laid by Mr. W. E. Bale, J.P., Hon. President, in the presence of a large and influential gathering ; and on the 2nd March, this year, the new premises were opened by His Excellency the Hon. Sir W. F. Hely-Hutchinson, G.C.M.G.

The President occupied the chair, and was supported by Colonel Hay, R.A., and a number of leading citizens.

The additions and alterations consist of a storey above the main hall, two new stories extending the frontage to the street line, and a number of rooms at the rear. On the ground floor are two shops and an office. Opening into the spacious corridor, which leads to the main hall, are the General Secretary's office, class and cloak rooms, and a lavatory.

A well-appointed staircase leads to the upper floor. Here are the parlour, library, reading-room, smoking-room, and refreshment bar. A handsome covered balcony gives a view of a large portion of the City and surrounding country. The boarding department consists of twelve large bed-sitting rooms, lavatories, three bath-rooms, dining-room, kitchen, stores, and matron's quarters.

At the rear, behind the Gymnasium, a stable, coach-house, and bicycle shed have been provided.

Increased seating accommodation has also been obtained for the main hall.

The premises throughout are lighted by electricity.

The whole of the additions have been designed and carried out in a most complete manner under the supervision of Mr. William Lucas, Architect, at a cost of £3,000.

The operations of the Association are divided into evangelistic, temperance, literary, recreative, and social.

The evangelistic agencies comprise on Sundays three meetings on the premises, with an aggregate attendance chiefly young men, of about 350, and two services, through the courtesy of Major-General Cox, at the Military Camp. A fortnightly service of sung is held at Grey's Hospital, and a monthly service at the Gaol.

A mission band conducts occasional services in outlying districts, and an annual service is conducted in the Town Hall.

Temperance work comprises a meeting every Saturday evening, after which pledges are taken. Allied to this section is an excellent choir. Efforts are also made to keep in personal touch with those who suffer from the drink curse.

Literary efforts are put forth in several directions, the chief being educational classes, lectures, and a debating society.

The reading room is kept well supplied with Home and Colonial papers and periodical literature. The circulating library consists of about 700 volumes The recreative and social committee is continually occupied in social gatherings for the members, regiments stationed in the City, or the public. Chess, draughs, bagatelle, and smoking-rooms have their patrons. An occasional medical talk is given. The Gymnasium is used, though not so extensively as it might be, by young men generally and social pupils.

The Association club room is granted gratuitously to the various athletic clubs in the City, and extensively used for periodical business meetings.

Another feature of the Y.M.C.A. movement, and in some respects the greater, consists in its freedom to take the initiative in general movements of social well-being.

Practical assistance is rendered in the direction of employment for young men, guidance as to suitable boarding houses, the visitation of the civilian and military hospitals, the granting of night shelter to the stranger in straitened circumstances.

The several rooms of the Association are freely placed at the disposal of various religious and philantropic societies that meet in congress in the City from time to time.

The United Evangelistic Committee and the Pietermaritzburg Temperance Union are in close co-operation with the Association.

Corresponding members exist throughout the Colony, in the Orange Free State and Rhodesia, and a proposal has been set on foot to establish district associations.

A branch of the Young Women's Christian Association was established in April, 1896, on the initiative of the Y.M.C.A., and has since then met on the Association premises. As tangible evidence of cordial relationship, the members' parlour in the new additions has been handsomely furnished as a gift from the Young Women.

A third feature of this movement is that it forms a platform of church representatives, lay and clerical ; in fact, a council of the churches of the City, uttering the voice of common Christianity in a manner impossible to any single sect, and, when necessary, taking such aggressive action as shall conserve the forces of the respective Churches.

In an association so multiform finance necessarily demands close attention, and this it certainly secures at the hands of Mr. J. Deverneuil, the Hon. Treasurer. The revenue is derived from members' fees, donations, subscriptions, the letting of rooms, and a private guarantee fund. It has long been felt, however, that by and under co-operation on the part of the City merchants, the civil servants, and citizens generally, far more could be accomplished in the development of the young manhood of Natal. Avoiding extremes, " on the one hand, the depraved desecrator who urges that ' Christian ' should be eradicated from the name, the Bible thrown out of the window, and the pool ball and poker chip introduced; and on the other hand, the misguided devotionalist who demands the purging of the temple, the closing of the Gymnasium, shutting up the reading room, banishing sociality, and permitting nothing but plain chairs, bare walls, and a perpetual high-pressure prayer meeting," the Pietermaritzburg Young Men's Christian Association seeks to benefit the whole man, physically, socially, educationally, and spiritually.

Mr. A. W. Frodsham, late of Lovedale, Cape Colony, is General Secretary, and the membership roll numbers about 220, including associates.

The annual subscription is £1; apprentices and young men under 18, 10s.

The people of Maritzburg owe a deep debt of gratitude to Mr. D. B. Scott, jun., for the magnificient Theatre which, at a considerable cost, he has caused to be erected in the City.

It required no small amount of courage to carry out an undertaking which, in the opinion of many people, was far in advance of the City's requirements.

The confidence in Maritzburg's progress displayed by Mr. Scott has already been justified, and it is now no idle boast to say that the Thespian goddess is provided in Maritzburg with a temple which will compare favourably with any in South Africa.

The structure, which is built in a modern style of architecture, was erected under Mr. Scott's personal supervision by Mr. H. K. McDowell, on modified plans originally prepared by Messrs. Street-Wilson and Fyfe, of Durban.

The builder, and the several artists employed on the premises, are to be congratulated on the perfect taste of the decoration, and the general success which has attended their labours.

The Story of an African City. 91

The structure occupies an area of about 130 by 130 feet, and consists of a tessalated hall, the Theatre itself, thirteen dressing rooms, two elaborate staircases with special carvings, and numerous corridors. Every provision has been made for the safety of the public, all ceilings and staircases being protected by asbestos.

On the ground floor there are seventeen exits, while the stage is fronted by a fireproof asbestos screen.

SCOTT'S THEATRE.

The Theatre is capable of accommodating about 1,500 persons at a stretch, but 1,000 can be comfortably seated.

There are nine boxes, luxuriantly fitted up, one of which, surmounted by the Royal Arms, is reserved for the Governor, and has attached to it a private sitting-room.

The height of the body of the Theatre is 30 feet, surmounted by a glass sliding dome roof.

The seats are made on the tilt-up principle, being of perforated wood to suit the hot climate.

The stage measurements are as follows :—Fifty feet by 35 feet ground measurement, and 66 feet from ground line to roof.

The building is lighted by 600 incandescent lights, the electrical installation having been carried out by Messrs. Siemens Brothers, of London.

THE STAGE, SCOTT'S THEATRE.

The scenery and all artistic necessaries for the stage are from the gifted brush of Mr. W. H. Thorne, while the figure studies over the proscenium are by Mr. Paton, of Durban.

Taken on the whole, the structure would do no discredit to any European City, and companies on tour will find all the latest and most modern improvements ready to hand, and those who have had experience of the stage accommodation in the old Theatre Royal will, we feel certain, fully endorse our opening remarks with reference to the public-spiritedness of Mr. D. B. Scott.

Local industries of some magnitude are now beginning to make their appearance in the City.

The Natal Tanning Company, Limited, deserves special mention, as it is the pioneer of an important class of industry which we hope to see flourish in Natal.

The company was incorporated in the year 1891. Its leather is produced from Natal hides, and is manufactured from Colonial-grown wattle bark.

The capital of the company is £8,000 ; it has earned the Government reward which was offered for the manufacture of Colonial leather.

It employs in all about 25 hands ; skilled Europeans operatives, Coolies, and Kafirs.

The premises, extending over five acres, are on the banks of the Umsindusi, where the company has ample water power for working all its machinery, grinding its bark, and pumping its liquors.

The machinery was all manufactured by Messrs. Huxham and Brown, of Exeter, and includes disintegrating, scouring, rolling, and belt-making machines.

The output of the Tannery is about 80 hides per week. These are converted into sole leather, harness leather, and machine belting.

The tan pits are 40 in number, and are, together with the adjoining lime pits, built of brick, lined with cement, and roofed over to protect them from storms.

The warehouses, drying and currying sheds are extensive. The quality of the company's leather has been steadily improving, and its sale gradually progressing.

The tan yard has been so planned that the number of pits can be doubled when occasion requires.

The cultivation of wattle (Acacia Mollisima) has now become one of the permanent industries of the Colony, and the supply of ox-hides is abundant.

In addition to wattle bark, the company uses other tanning ingredients, such as sumach, salonia, and myrabolane, which it has to import at present, but which could all be grown in this Colony.

No expense is being spared to produce a leather that will compare favourably with that imported from Britain.

The Natal Brewery must be regarded as one of the most successful enterprises of the City.

Originally a syndicate, founded by Mr. Frederick Mead, with a registered capital of £30,000, it steadily justified the hopes centred on it by its promoters, and the operations commenced in 1890 were of so satisfactory a character as to necessitate very considerable enlargements, both as regards capital and premises.

In 1893 the syndicate was re-constructed. the new company having a capital of £130,000. In addition to carrying out extensive improvements at the Maritzburg Brewery, the Castle Brewery at Johannesburg was purchased. As the latter had to be practically re-built, increased capital was necessary, and the company was again floated under the name of the "South African Breweries, Limited," with a paid-up capital of £455,000. Of this sum £100,000 have been sunk in the Natal Brewery, and about £60,000 is at the present time invested in other ways in the Colony of Natal.

The present plant of the Natal Brewery is capable of turning out from 600 to 700 barrels of beer, each of 36 gallons, per week. The total storage capacity of the premises is about 1,500 barrels, besides beer contained in vats and tuns.

About 50 white men and 60 natives are employed by the company.

The success of the Brewery has been almost phenomenal, which is shown by the fact that for the year ending March 31st, 1895, the company was able to declare a dividend of 15 per cent., while for the last financial year a dividend of 12½ per cent. was paid on a capital of very nearly half-a-million.

The South African Breweries, Limited, is controlled by a board of directors in London, of which Mr. Hackblock, a well-known Norwich brewer, is Chairman, and Mr. Frederick Mead, Deputy Chairman.

There is also a Johannesburg board of directors, who have to deal with the branch brewery there, but who exercise no control over the Maritzburg concern.

The manager of the Natal Brewery is Mr. C. A. Chidell, a gentleman who has been connected with the concern since its commencement, and who four years ago was transferred to Natal. Mr. A. J. Day, whose skill and experience are well-known in the trade, is the head brewer.

The brewery and plant are of the most modern and complete design, and it is generally conceded that the beers brewed in Maritzburg are the best manufactured in South Africa. The credit is due to this company of introducing to South Africa the screw-stoppered bottle, which of late years has become so popular in Great Britain.

The Agricultural Show which is held in Pietermaritzburg annually during the month of May is an important feature in the industry and progress of the Colony. Exhibits of every description of produce, manufactures, implements, cattle, dogs, poultry, etc., are received from all parts of Natal, and valuable prizes, presented by individuals, as well as by the Society, are awarded to the successful competitors. It has increased year by year, and is now the most flourishing of its kind in South Africa.

The Hon. T. K. Murray, Esq., M.L.A., who for a considerable time was President of the Society, has by his indefatigable energy, contributed most materially to its success.

The able and energetic Secretary, Mr. A. Whittle Herbert, has placed the agricultural community of Maritzburg deeply in his debt, for its progress and present important standing is mainly due to his methodical management and organisation.

The extensive property, to which additions have recently been made, and a large hall in the grounds are sufficient testimony to the growing importance of this institution.

The Horticultural Society is also worthy of mention. It was established in the year 1864, and had for its object the encouragement of the growth of indigenous and exotic flora, fruits, and vegetables.

The Society holds five or six exhibitions throughout the Colony every year. It is self-supporting, and has done eminent service in the direction aimed at by its founders.

In concluding these remarks on the public institutions, buildings, and industries of the City, it is necessary to mention the Natal Bank, Limited, as one of Natal's most successful financial enterprises.

It was established in 1854, incorporated in 1859, and is now incorporated under the Natal Bank, Limited, Law of 1888. Its head offices are in the City, and it has branches throughout Natal, Transvaal, Zululand, and London, the latter branch being located at 156 and 157, Leadenhall Street, E.C. The authorised capital is £2,000,000, subscribed capital £878,110, paid-up capital £284,237 10s., and its reserve fund £45,000. It is the official bank of the Government.

The Standard Bank of South Africa, Limited, and the Bank of Africa, Limited, have also important branches in the City.

Maritzburg possesses at the present time five journals and several magazines. The *Natal Witness*, published every morning; the *Times of Natal*, every evening; the *Natal Afrikaner*, published twice a week in the Dutch language; the *Government Gazette* weekly; and the *Government Agricultural Journal*, which is published fortnightly.

Elsewhere in this volume the date of the establishment of the first-named journal is mentioned. The *Times of Natal* dates from 1851, and was first published in Durban.

CHAPTER XV.

Maritzburg as a Health Resort.—Vital Statistics.—Effect of Climate on Diseases.—Pleasure Resorts.

VILLAGE OF HOWICK.

IN order to arrive at the actual truth with regard to Maritzburg's status as a health resort, we resolved, instead of depending merely on common report or personal impressions, to endeavour to obtain from the Health Officer of the Borough as complete a statement as possible on a subject of such vital importance.

Accordingly we called on that popular official, and in the course of an hour's conversation, elicited the following information.

Before proceeding to deal with it, it may be of interest to distant readers to know that Dr. James F. Allen, M.D, M.Ch.M.L., R.U.I., came to Natal in 1874, and settled in Maritzburg.

Since his arrival, he has grown steadily in popularity, and can now, with all justice, be described as one of the first medical practitioners in South Africa. He was President of the third South African Medical Congress, and has contributed in various ways to the scientific and general literature of the day.

TUGELA FALLS, COLENSO.

Having resided for so long in Maritzburg in the active practice of his profession, there are few, if any, who are better qualified to deal with the vital statistics of the place.

Not only is he Visiting Surgeon to Grey's Hospital, and to many educational institutions, in this City, but he is Medical Officer to the Corporation.

In response to our request for information, he readily afforded us the full benefit of his wide and varied experience

In reply to a question as to whether Maritzburg is a desirable place to seek by those in quest of health, he said : — It cannot be said of any place that it is a perfect health resort all the year round ; still there are certain facts which are indisputable, and which may be used as gauges for comparison, as for example, the local death rate. This record does not tell everything, but it is nevertheless a good general guide to the healthiness of a place.

GIANT ALOES.

Taking the past five years together, the average death rate of this town has been 13.5 per thousand per annum ; but the death rate is not an altogether reliable guide ; it is more desirable, if possible, to arrive at the sick rate, *i.e* , the prevalence of diseases of a non-fatal character which might give a place a bad health record without affecting its death rate.

One way in which this can be done, approximately, is by comparing it with other places in respect of the number of medical men it employs. Doctors are not likely to stay in a place too healthy to support them. These matters tend to balance themselves, and in doing so produce a register from which fairly correct deductions can be made.

In London, which is considered one of the healthiest cities in the world, there is one medical practitioner to every 750 inhabitants, whereas in Maritzburg it takes at least 3,000 persons to support one doctor. It must be borne in mind that the death returns, as shown in the City rate, are much higher than should actually apply to residents, there being a tendency for sick and failing people to come to the City for medical advice, and, of course, among such persons the death rate is high, and their record is placed to the town's account, thereby considerably raising it by the register of the deaths of persons who do not actually reside here, and who have succumbed to diseases contracted elsewhere, and which, of course, have no local bearing.

There is also a general hospital and a large lunatic asylum which, in each case, receives patients from all parts of Natal, the Orange Free State, the Transvaal Republic, and Portuguese East Africa. Thus it is evident that there are many extraneous sources which tend to swell the death rate above what is normal to Maritzburg.

The climate of the City and its suburbs is so healthy that, even with these additions to the death rate, it can still show a record which will compare favourably with any town or community of the same size in the United Kingdom, and most favourably with any similar town in South Africa.

This is specially instructive in our case, because as far as I know Maritzburg is the only City in South Africa that has the courage to publish complete returns; that is, to take the population as a whole, white and coloured, without regard to the actual place of domicile.

In other lands possessing more complete and extensive statistical machinery, vital statistics are kept more correctly than in South Africa. Errors which occur here are guarded against, as, for instance, if a London resident goes to Brighton and dies there, his death is registered, not where he

CASCADE, TOWN BUSH VALLEY

died, but where he lived; here it is invariably where he dies. In time this will be changed, but at present such a course is not possible. Many things are favourable to life in this City, and therefore contribute to lower the death rate. The most important being that we have no epidemic diseases, and malaria, the endemic disease of other parts of Africa, is unknown.

The situation of the town is about faultless, it being thoroughly sheltered on the north and west, from the former of which directions come the most trying winds of South Africa, and from the latter the rains and storms.

The town is built on a ridge falling gently on all sides, and draining into streams which carry off the surface water, so that in a few hours after rain has ceased the ground is dry and clean. At present our Corporation is carrying out a plan to systematically improve the natural drainage.

The citizens live much of their lives in the open air; there is a beautiful, well-planted Park, in which driving, riding, and games, such as cricket and football, can be, and are, extensively enjoyed.

We are fortunate enough to have an ample supply of excellent drinking water and to possess a handsome public bath, the latter the gift of one of our leading townsmen, which is a great benefit to the place.

There is a considerable difference between life in the English towns and life in the City of Maritzburg, for here there are far greater opportunities of enjoying the open air, which is always conducive to the maintenance of good health and long life.

No doubt we have storms and heat, and both at times keep us indoors, but neither last long, and great heat is invariably followed by rain, and a consequent fall in the temperature. The rain seldom lasts for more than a day, and for the most part only for a few hours. The weather in the City does not continually occupy people's minds and thoughts If one is going out it is not the all-absorbing topic, nor is it the marsport that it is in England.

We know that, however inopportune it may be, it will not last long, and we can depend upon having more good than bad.

There are many other attractions which invite people to reside here, a fine Theatre, a well-filled Library and Museum, and last, though not least, a Garrison of about 2,000 British troops.

All these tend to make life happy and secure. Maritzburg is also the capital of the Colony, and the seat of Government; its schools are of a very high standard, and

ALBERT FALLS, RIVER UMGENI.

the town is steadily obtaining a first-class reputation as one of the most important educational centres in South Africa.

Touching the health of the public and boarding schools, the record is phenomenal, and perhaps more than anything else shows what a really healthy place the City is. During last year, which was by no means an exceptionally good one from a health point of view, there was not a single case of really serious illness in any of the schools which I have the privilege to attend, and when I tell you that the resident pupils of both sexes under my care total about 400, some idea of the value of this statement as a health record may be grasped.

This state of affairs is no exception, it is the normal standard. Boys and girls in this climate can enjoy the same sports and pastimes as occupy them in England; the boys have cricket and football, and the girls tennis, while both fly about on bicycles. Every disease here takes a milder form than in England; indeed it would be hard to find any complaint which is more virulent here than there. This especially applies to the diseases of children, such as scarlatina, measles, whooping cough, and chicken-pox.

In Europe some of these are most dangerous and fatal complaints, but here the naturally increased action of the skin, the result of a comparatively warm climate, seems to mitigate their severity. This has an important bearing on the general health of the country. In Europe very frequently it is the occurrence of one or other of these diseases during childhood that prepares the way for graver complaints in after life, and especially makes people susceptible to consumption. I can safely say that in this City, with whose mortuary statistics I am familiar, the death rate from these diseases is practically *nil*, and that recovery takes place without any constitutional impairment.

Regarding Maritzburg as a suitable place for invalids, I do not think that it is to the advantage of any place to become a regular resort for invalids. Not that I would deny the sick and weak any of the benefits of our climate, or rather our climates. What is more to be desired is that healthy families should be domiciled here, and should enjoy the advantages of our town as a place of residence.

Invalids do come, as it is, in limited numbers; but, unfortunately, so far, most of them are either too advanced in disease, especially consumption, to recover, or else they are too poor to get the full benefit of our climate. By the well-to-do, South Africa as a health resort is neglected, or

LION'S RIVER FALLS.

rather has scarcely been discovered, and medical practitioners who advise people to come here for health reasons are, generally speaking, not sufficiently acquainted with the variations of our climate or the configuration of the country. They are guided mainly by the altitudes of the places to which they send patients; although no doubt this is in many forms of disease a good guide to a suitable place of residence in South Africa, it is often misleading. In the higher parts of the southern continent of Africa there is little or no shelter, and consequently in the winter, places at high elevations are generally exposed to cold winds and dust-storms, both having a most injurious effect on those suffering from lung complaints.

The fact is that our climate has never yet been taken advantage of, on any extensive scale, by persons suffering from lung affections, for the reason that but few come here who have the means to live in such a manner as to derive the greatest good from the climate. As I have said, most of the people who seek health here are those who must also make their living, the result is that they are compelled to reside all the year around in one locality. The consequences being that in a number of cases the sufferers lose in the summer in places of low altitude what they have gained in the winter, and in the higher places the benefit they get in the summer is lost if they stay the winter. Nothing, of course, can alter this; as far as the poor are concerned they must live where they can earn their bread. For those who can afford it, the best way in which to get the fullest benefits from our climate is to move up to the highlands in summer, and return to the more sheltered places in winter, at which season of the year no place in South Africa affords greater attractions as a health resort than Maritzburg, that is to say, from the 1st of April to the 30th September.

The town being so much better sheltered from dust-storms and high winds than the more bleak plains, makes it in a marked degree a desirable residential place.

In addition to congenial society, it is within easy railway reach of the sea and the high level plateaux, so that when it becomes generally known there is no doubt but that many families, not only invalids, but others, will seek health and prolonged life in the City. Another important fact which should not be overlooked is that every successive generation of delicate people appears to improve in health and physique.

Maritzburg offers especial attractions to those delicate persons who are not actually suffering from consumption or other chest disease, but who are predisposed in that direction. Persons of this class can live in our City all the year round with benefit. The altitude above the sea of the City itself is 2,218 feet, and as I have already said, just outside the town there is a range of hills facing the south-east and attaining an altitude of from 2,900 to 3,000 feet. This range faces the south-east, from which direction the cool winds come. Dotted about in sheltered nooks in these altitudes many comfortable homes have been made. It has been found that nearly every variety of pine, fir, oak, and wattle flourish luxuriantly. It is no uncommon sight to see houses originally placed on a bare slope, in the course of a few years surrounded with ornamental and fruit trees.

This raises another important thought which may be mentioned, although it has actually nothing to do with Maritzburg from the health aspect, and that is the cultivation of orange and lemon trees.

I firmly believe that this industry would prove to be not only healthy, but most remunerative, as the demands for both the fruit and its extracts is steadily increasing throughout the country.

All that is required is industry and intelligent cultivation to make, not only the City, but the Colony of Natal the "Riviera of South Africa."

The foregoing remarks will be read with special interest as coming from one who is thoroughly acquainted, not only with the City itself, but with the rest of South Africa.

With the Railway sweeping throughout the length of the land, hundreds of attractive resorts, both for health and pleasure are easily attainable in a few hours' journey. For instance, the wild and broken scenery of Inchanga, Botha's Hill, and Krantz Kloof, lying between Maritzburg and Durban can be reached within two hours by rail, while in the opposite direction many charming health resorts are to be found at Mooi River, Nottingham Road, and elsewhere.

Should the sojourner in Maritzburg so desire it, he may in about half a day, visit the stately pinnacles of the Drakens-

HEAD OF HOWICK FALLS.

berg, saunter beside the tawny waves of the Tugela at Colenso, or visit the tragic scenes of the Weenen massacre.

Turning our attention more particularly to the health and pleasure resorts of Maritzburg proper, we have first on our list, the beautiful village of Howick.

The falls of the Umgeni River at this place are generally admitted to be one of the most interesting sights of its kind in Africa. The stream, which is a considerable one, speeds down from the uplands in a series of beautiful cascades, until it reaches the chasm, over which it is hurled in a sheer fall of 365 feet. The roar of the cataract, the deep pool below it, the whirling rapids beyond, combined with the grand scenery, tend to make up a panorama which is difficult to adequately describe. Capital hotel accommodation

HOWICK FALLS.

is provided in the village, and everything is done to secure the comfort and pleasure of visitors.

In the immediate vicinity of the City, there are the Park, the Town Bush, and Chase Valleys, while Sweetwaters and Winterskloof are favourite picnic resorts. The

palm for grandeur of scenery must be given to the Table
Mountain district, situated fourteen miles by road from the
City. Here the tourist may, by a limited expenditure of
money and energy, fully enjoy a peep at as dense barbarism
as ever prevailed in the interior of the Continent. The wild
mountains, with their deep forests of palms and ferns, still

A SPUR OF TABLE MOUNTAIN.

echo the booming bark of the baboon or the plaintive howl
of the hyaena. Native chieftains hold their courts there, and
the Zulu chant, now shorn of its terrors, may yet be heard.
Not only is this district eminently beautiful, but it teems
with interest to the scientific student, nearly every description of rock, from recent shale to the most ancient formation,
can be discovered in the scarred mountain slopes, towering

here and there. The fantastic hills appear at times to be almost enchanted, and when in the early dawn, through the rolling clouds of mist, their giant forms emerge, one can fully realise how it came about that travellers' tales are some-

A ZULU.

times doubted, for to attempt anything like an accurate word picture of the majesty and beauty of the scene would be almost to court the disbelief of those who have not visited the locality.

The Albert Falls, on the Umgeni, which are to be seen on the Greytown road, are about fourteen miles out of Maritzburg, and constitute the most attractive feature in the neighbourhood. They are thought, by most people, to give more satisfaction than those at Howick, which they surpass in volume, the river here being, of course, somewhat larger. Though the water has to descend a much shorter distance than at Howick, the falls more than make up what grandeur they lose in the matter of height by their great width. Gazing at the water as it comes tumbling over, to go swirling past in a miniature Niagara rapids, one easily gains the impression of there being a dozen waterfalls side by side, divided by towering masses of rugged lichen-covered rocks, crowned with clumps of trees, which, with the other surrounding foliage, the brown and grey stone, the foam-flecked, hurrying stream, the falling water, and the bright sunshine, form a picture not easily forgotten. Above the falls is a stretch of river, eight miles in length, suitable for rowing and sailing, on which are several boats for the convenience of visitors. This and other easily-accessible portions of the river give excellent fishing and shooting. The place is already receiving an increasing number of visitors from town, and only needs the completion of the railway to attain a much larger degree of popularity. The " Waterfall " Hotel, situated some 12 miles from Maritzburg beyond, is composed of a substantial building, which has been renovated, and of a number of rooms which are being added. Stables are in the course of erection, and a good roadway is about to be made to the falls, and to the fishing and boating waters above, of which there are about fourteen miles.

CHAPTER XVI.

Education Statistics.—Mr. Robert Russell.—Maritzburg College.—Blenheim School.—Girls' Collegiate School.—Thanet House School.

IN approaching the important subject of education, we think it is advisable, as this book will probably find its way into the hands of many readers who can have had no opportunity of making themselves acquainted with official Blue Book returns, to deal with the question from a State point of view first, and then proceed to the consideration of Maritzburg itself as an educational centre. The advantage of such a course is that it affords a standard of comparison, not only for the Colony of Natal, but for the rest of South Africa as well.

It will be seen by those who take the trouble to analyse and compare the Natal returns with those of the other States of South Africa that, in proportion to its population, it in many respects takes a leading place. In connection both with the system adopted and the selection of those who administer it, the Government and the Municipalities have spared neither expense nor effort in this all-important department.

Although the Colony is a British one, it possesses a heavy percentage of Dutch settlers in the uplands, and the Government, in order to meet the requirements of all classes, has provided full facilities for imparting instruction in the Dutch language, an Inspector being specially retained for this purpose.

Up to the year 1865, Government supported one High School for boys and two Primary Schools for boys and girls, besides giving aid to about 60 schools scattered throughout the Colony. From that date onwards it was the aim of the Government to establish more Government Schools, and to extend aid to all schools complying with certain conditions.

By the end of 1877, four schools, two High and two Primary, one of each in Pietermaritzburg and Durban, had been established and were maintained and managed entirely by the Government, the Governor through the Superintendent of Education having the immediate control. In both town and country, other schools established by committees or private individuals, and varying annually in number from 5 to 91, were aided by Government with grants from £16 to £136 a year each.

To put educational matters under the guidance of a special Council, and to systematise into law the general principles and conditions which should regulate educational action, two Bills were framed by the Governor and passed by the Legislative Council in 1877, the one to make better provision for primary or elementary education, and the other to promote secondary education.

On January 1st, 1878, the Council of Education assumed its duties, and after 16½ years' good work, it was abolished by the Education Act of 1894, which virtually vested the powers of the Council in the Minister of Education, with the Superintendent of Education as Chief Executive Officer.

Various improvements are being gradually effected in the work and regulations of the Department. It is the endeavour of the Government to bring education within easy reach of every European child in the Colony, and to provide facilities, as far as practicable, for giving a suitable training to the children of Natives and Indians.

Although education is for the most part controlled by the Government, there are a good many schools, both primary and secondary, which are not under inspection. These private schools are mostly doing excellent work.

The European population is about 50,000, and the number of children at school is about 9,600. This is very nearly one-fifth, the usual estimated proportion being one-sixth, and there seems to be no need for a compulsory Act. Government provides free education to all who are not able to pay the school fees. There are probably not more than 200 children of school age who are not receiving schooling of some kind. These figures refer only to the white population.

The Native population numbers about 500,000, and the Indian population about 50,000. The latter were imported as labourers on plantations and farms, and those of them whose term of indenture has expired are occupied as small storekeepers, market-gardeners, fishermen, hawkers, and domestic servants.

The Executive Branch of the Educational Department consists of the Minister of Education (Hon. Henry Bale, Q.C., M.L.A.), Superintendent of Education (Mr. Robert Russell), two Assistant Inspectors (Messrs. C. J. Mudie and J. H Kleinschmidt), an Inspector of Native Education (Mr. R. Plant), an Inspector of Indian Schools (Mr. F. Colepeper), the Clerk and Accountant (Mr. W. H. Bennett), and a Statistical Clerk (Mr. J. Austin).

The Science, Art, and Technical Department is under the charge of Major S. Herbert, who is assisted by two Art Masters, one at Maritzburg (Mr. C. E. Chidley), and the other at Durban (Mr. W. H. T. Venner).

An annual *viva voce* examination of each school is held, the date being fixed by the Inspectors, sufficient notification being given to the head teacher. All schools receiving Government aid are open at any time to the Officers of the Education Department, and visits without notice are made by all Inspectors. As far as possible the Inspectorial and clerical staffs are appointed from the ranks of the teachers.

In 1897 there were 508 schools under Government inspection—319 European schools, 159 Native schools, and 30 Indian schools—with an aggregate attendance of 19,222

(10,075 boys and 9,147 girls), consisting of 7,685 Europeans (4,099 boys and 3,586 girls); 8,542 Natives (3,580 boys and 4,962 girls); and 2,995 Indians (2,396 boys and 599 girls).

The average regular daily attendance is in European schools 87 per cent. of the number enrolled; in Native schools 75 per cent.; and in Indian schools 80 per cent.

The number present at the annual inspections was 7,129 Europeans, 5,209 Natives, and 1,562 Indians. It is estimated that about 1,600 children of European parentage are being taught privately or at schools not in receipt of Government aid.

Of the 508 schools, 23 have been established and are maintained exclusively by Government. All the other schools are either private schools, denominational schools, or board schools, receiving grants in aid varying from £10 to £250 a year each.

Nearly all the Native and Indians schools are directly connected with the various religious bodies in the Colony.

The Government Schools consist of two High Schools, four Model Schools, 13 Primary Schools, two Art Schools, and two Indian Schools.

Maritzburg and Durban have each one High School and two Model Schools. One of the Primary Schools is in Maritzburg, one at Addington (a suburb of Durban), and the other eleven are country schools established in the chief centres of population.

The work of the two High Schools is based on the Matriculation and the B A. Intermediate examinations of the Cape University. The Headmasters nominate their own assistants, and they are left almost entirely free in everything relating to the work and management of their schools. The aggregate attendance is about 225, and accommodation is provided for 100 boarders.

An Exhibition to a Home University of £150 a year, tenable for four years, is given annually. One of the exhibitioners, Mr. T. J. Bromwich, was Senior Wrangler in 1895, and his distinguished success was a source of much gratification to the Colony.

There is also a Mining Scholarship of £80 a year for four years, given on certain conditions to the boy who passes highest in the Cape University Intermediate Examination, provided he obtains satisfactory marks in Mathematics.

There are also four Bursaries of £40 a year and six Bursaries of £20 a year for three years, given on certain conditions to the ten pupils who stand highest in the Bursary Examination. The higher Bursaries are limited to pupils outside Maritzburg and Durban, and the successful candidates will attend a boarding school approved by the Minister of Education.

The collective attendance at the four Model Schools is about 2,200. The majority of the head teachers and the chief assistants of these schools and of the country schools are British trained, and their work is modelled on that of the best British schools.

From time to time, teachers holding the British Privy Council certificate have been selected by accredited persons in Britain and sent out to senior posts, but promotion to juniors who have served well and faithfully is the guiding principle in the majority of appointments Teaching as a profession is not popular with the colonial lad, but girls can be had without difficulty.

There is a pupil teacher system similar to that of Britain. The pupil teacher is nominated from the best senior pupils, and the nomination is approved or disapproved of by the Superintendent of Education.

The apprenticeship extends over four years, and the apprentices are examined annually by the Department. The proportion of male to female teachers is 7—12.

The Education Department has been made an integral part of the Civil Service of the Colony since August, 1898.

The books, furniture, and apparatus are all modern. Cookery schools are attached to the two girls' Model Schools, and workshops and science classes to the two boys' Model Schools and to most of the country schools.

The two Art Schools are in charge of teachers certificated from South Kensington, and the students take part in the various British drawing, science, and technical examinations. The Director of the Art School exercises a control over the science and technical work of all the Government Schools. The European schools are divided into fixed and farm schools.

There are 67 of the former and 252 of the latter. The farm-school system was established in 1887 for the benefit of the children of farmers and others in sparsely-peopled districts.

They may come up for examination to the nearest Government School, or an Inspector will visit any house where not fewer than ten pupils can be gathered together, provided that such examination centre is not less than five miles from a Government or Aided School.

The grant of £3 a year is made for every pupil who is able to show satisfactory progress The syllabus of instruction is almost indentical with that of the Government Schools.

The total ordinary expenditure for 1897 amounted to £45,457, divided thus :— Europeans, £38,007 ; Natives, £5,528 ; Indians, £1,922.

The average cost to the Government for educating each child is about £2 6s. 2d.—each European child costing

£3 13s. 6d., each Native child 17s. 10s., and each Indian child 18s 9d. This charge includes all expenses of administration. The Government cost per head at the High Schools is about £9 17s., at the Model Schools £3 17s., at the Country Schools £7 14s., at the Aided Schools £2, and at the Farm Schools £3 8s. Special provision is made in all the Government Schools for instruction in Dutch.

The salaries of the head teachers range from £300 to £550 per annum, and of assistants from £80 to £300 per annum.

The revenue derived from Government School fees in 1897 amounted to £7,532 16s. from Europeans, and £42 17s. 3d. from Indians. The rate of fees varies from 1s. to 5s. a month at the Model and Primary Schools, and from 10s. to £1 a month at the High Schools. Boarders pay from £30 to £60 a year each.

Education in the Government Schools is to all intents and purposes secular and unsectarian. The following re religious instruction appears in the rules to be followed in Government Schools :—" School shall be opened with prayer. Regular religious instruction of a simple and unsectarian kind shall be given throughout the school, but any scholar may be withdrawn by his or her parent or guardian from such instruction without forfeiting any of the other benefits of the school."

All Government School buildings are erected and maintained by the Public Works Department.

There is a library attached to every Government School. Calisthenics, drill, and singing form an important part of every curriculum Two thousand boys have been formed into a regiment of Cadets, and twelve hundred of these are armed and able to shoot. A collective encampment is held annually for four or five days.

The general principle adopted is to secure the best teachers, and to give them a free hand. They are allowed to follow their own methods.

The children of the colonists are all well fed and well clothed. There is no necessity for providing free dinners, nor for Reformatory or Industrial Schools.

Blind people and persons of defective intelligence are rarely met with, and the school in Durban for deaf and dumb, which costs Government £400 per annum, has only eight pupils.

Evening classes in science, shorthand, etc., have been established in connection with the Government Schools, and have met with considerable success.

Mr. Robt. Russell, who is now the permanent and responsible head of the educational system of Natal, came to the Colony in 1865, he having been appointed by the Secretary of State for the Colonies to take charge of the Government High School then about to be established in Durban.

A similar institution had already been successfully inaugurated in Maritzburg. Not only was the necessity of such an establishment urgently felt at the Port, but it was also considered advisable that the official selected to take charge of it should be highly qualified and experienced.

At the time of Mr. Russell's selection for the post he was a student at Edinburgh University, and Master of Method in the Church of Scotland Training College in the same ancient City.

When the appointment was offered to him he had the alternative of continuing at the University, where a brilliant career was opening before him, or of casting in his lot amongst strangers in a strange land. Fortunately for Natal he selected the latter alternative, and has ever since not only steadily grown in popularity, but has also exercised a potent influence on the intellectual and literary life of the Colony.

The Durban High School was opened on the 1st of June, 1866, and at once became under his control a popular and useful institution.

Its attendance, at first naturally meagre, steadily increased to 100, which, considering the numerical weakness of the town and district, and the utilitarian lives which the settlers had to lead, was justly considered a high percentage.

MR. R. RUSSELL, SUPERINTENDENT OF EDUCATION.

In January, 1875, Mr Russell was appointed Associate Inspector of Schools, and on the death of the Superintendent of Education, during the following year, he was appointed to succeed him.

In January, 1878, the Council of Education was created, and Mr. Russell's designation altered to that of Superintendent Inspector of Schools, while at the same time he was appointed Secretary of the newly - established Council.

In the former capacity he was held responsible to the Government for the proper administration of the funds set apart for educational purposes, and also for the conduct of the operations of the department.

When the Council of Education was abolished, four years ago (1894), Mr. Russell again became the permanent head of the Education Department under a Minister of Education.

In March. 1897, Natal became affiliated with the Cape University, and Mr. Russell was appointed one of the three members to represent the Colony on the University Council.

Throughout his career, both official and private, Mr. Russell has ever shown that breadth of view and adaptability to circumstance which are such essential qualifications in the chief of a department, whose duty it is to build up and strengthen the minds and characters of those who are destined to be the strength and support of a struggling and progressive country. In addition to the conscientious discharge of his onerous official duties, he has found time to produce that widely-known work, now in its sixth edition, " Natal : the Land and its Story." The careful research into the history of the country, as well as his lucid and able descriptions of its physical geography, stamp him as no mean figure in the literary history of Natal.

During a ten months' leave of absence in 1897, Mr. Russell visited schools of all descriptions in England and on the Continent. From what we could gather it would appear that the leave of absence was by no means a holiday trip, for the data collected by him is calculated to tell most beneficially on the work of his department.

When questioned as to his general impressions, it appeared that he had been pleasingly struck with the progress made on all sides in technical education ; for instance, he found a well-equipped Technical School in close proximity to the time-honoured University of Upsala in Sweden. At the same time he found that the Natal Government Primary and Secondary Schools compared not unfavourably with similar institutions in England and the Continent.

At a very large educational gathering held at Earl's Court under the auspices of the Society of Arts and the Countess of Warwick, Mr. Russell was deputed to speak on education in South Africa. No better choice of an exponent qualified to do justice to the theme could have been made.

It is to be hoped that Mr. Russell will long be spared in health and vigour to administer the affairs of his important department.

The Maritzburg College is entitled to take first rank as an educational institution, not only in the City but in the Colony.

It is scarcely necessary in these pages to trace the origin of the institution, or its connection with the Collegiate Trust, established under Law 18, 1861. Suffice it to say, that after six years of trial of the Government provisions for secondary or higher education, under Law 16 of 1877, it was felt that higher education was somehow not flourishing, and that a change must be effected.

Accordingly the matter was vigorously taken up by the Council of Education, which resulted in a Bill being presented to Parliament and ultimately passed as Law 45 of 1884.

This Law was entituled " To repeal in certain respects Law 18 of 1861, and to make provision for certain funds and lands under the said Law being made available for the educational needs of the Colony." In signing this Law, Sir Henry Bulwer, whose name will ever be prominently connected with the history of education in Natal, realised in a sense his cherished project of the establishment of an endowed Collegiate Institution or College.

The establishment is Collegiate in respect of its having young men in residence, who study for the Degree Examinations of the Cape of Good Hope University, with which it is thus affiliated.

MARITZBURG COLLEGE.

It also represents the High School in that, in the lower or preparatory school, elementary instruction is imparted.

The building is a stately one, which a reference to our illustration will show, and was constructed on plans furnished by the late Mr. Dudgeon, the Architect of the Durban Town Hall.

By the prolongation of the two projecting wings, a finely proportioned quadrangle is formed.

STAFF, MARITZBURG COLLEGE.

These flanking blocks contain on the ground floor the two largest class-rooms, the dining-room, and lavatories, and in the upper story the largest dormitories, the hospital, the laundry, and the servants' rooms.

Magnificient town and country views are obtainable everywhere from the College, but more especially from the upper windows.

The Masters' residences occupy either end of the main building.

The first object to catch the eye of the visitor is the entrance hall, with its massively-designed collonade and staircase leading to the library immediately above. On the right hand side of the entrance hall is a marble tablet, erected in memory of former pupils of the school who fell in battle in the defence of their country.

The College Library, in which there is a portrait of the late Dr. Mann, at one time Superintendent of Education in the Colony, is enriched by a generous donation from Mrs. Mann of a valuable collection of books, including the new edition of the "Encyclopædia Britannica," in handsome binding.

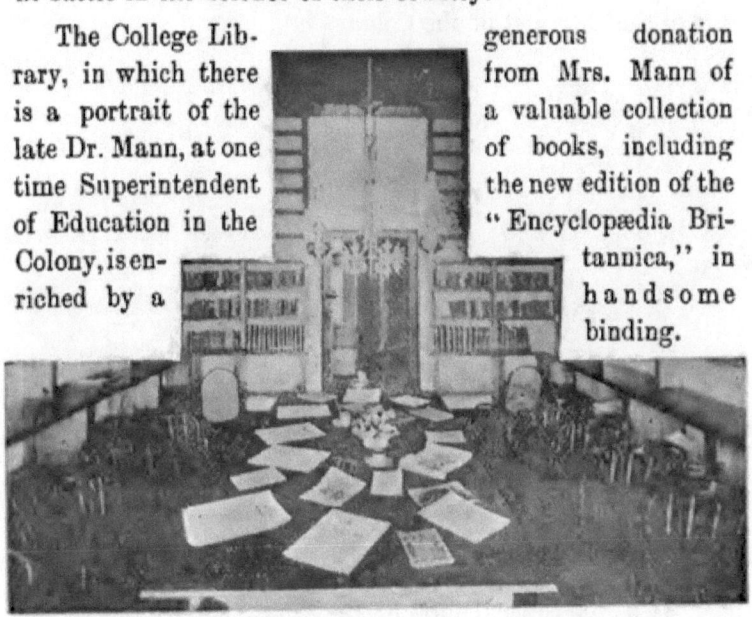

THE LIBRARY, MARITZBURG COLLEGE.

To the left of the staircase is the Masters' retiring room, and a reference library.

A lofty and airy corridor traverses the whole length of the upper story.

Since the opening of the College in August, 1888, considerable additions have been made to the staff, on which there are now highly qualified and eminent teachers in the department of classics, English literature, science, mathematics, and modern languages, holding high degrees from British and Continental Universities.

The Headmaster, Mr. R. D. Clark, M.A., of New College, and former Fellow and Tutor of Edinburgh University, also of the Inner Temple, Barrister-at-Law, is a gentleman who has, both as a distinguished scholar and a public-spirited Colonist, impressed his personality deeply, indelibly, and beneficially alike on the educational and social life of the City and of the Colony.

THE HEADMASTER IN HIS STUDY.

It is due to the efforts of Mr. Clark and his assistant Masters that a gratifying *esprit de corps* has been evoked in the College, by means of societies, cadet corps, and athletics, in which the College boys have won a reputation.

The following is a list of the staff of the College, who assist Mr. Clark in the arduous duties of the institution :— English Master, Rev. J. Stalker, M.A., Edinburgh University; Mathematical and Science Master, Mr. H. W. Graham, M.A., Cambridge; Professor of Modern Languages, Mr. H. Von Gerard, University of Würzburg; House

Masters, Messrs. A. S. Langley and C. T. Loram, Cape University; Art Instructor, Mr. C. E. Chidley, Natal Government Art School; Music Instructor, Mr. A. Campbell-Rowland; Military Drill and Gymnastics, Sergeant-Major Bowen, Natal Carbineers; Matron, Mrs. Richards.

In order that readers at a distance may grasp the full value of the College as a training centre, we incorporate here the rules and regulations which must be conformed to by students, and in doing so may state that they apply more

THE VESTIBULE, MARITZBURG COLLEGE.

or less to the various other educational establishments mentioned in this chapter.

RULES AND REGULATIONS.

1. Punctual attendance on the ringing of a bell for meals or study will be strictly enforced.

No hat is to be worn within the College, and there is to be no rushing, pushing, or shouting within the building or on the verandahs.

3. The inmate of one dormitory is on no account to enter any other.

4. Boys are specially reminded that the dormitories are solely for sleeping purposes; until bedtime they are to be entered only for good and sufficient reasons, and if a sick boy wishes to lie down on his bed he must first take off his boots. Lights are to be put out at 10.30 by the Prefects of the several dormitories.

5. The rule as to pushing, shouting, and horseplay will be stringently enforced in the dormitories, and for the strict observance of this rule, and of Rules Nos. 3 and 4, the Perfects, who have full powers in this matter, will be held responsible.

DINING ROOM, MARITZBURG COLLEGE.

6. Each boy is to make out accurately, in duplicate, on a sheet of notepaper, a weekly list of his washing, so as to check it when returned.

7. All dirty boots or shoes are to be placed in the boot-room before tea, at and after which meal slippers only may be worn, and no one thereafter may leave the main building except for necessary purposes.

8. Anyone entering the dining-room after grace has been said will be liable to an imposition.

9. Careless spilling of ink will in every case be severely punished.

10. All books, etc., used in the studies must be replaced in the owner's desk before he retires to rest.

11. Lamps must be brought down to the lamp-room before 9 a.m. on Mondays, Wednesdays, and Fridays and replaced and lighted before sunset

12. No boy may leave the College grounds without permission, save on Saturdays, and then only after dinner, from which time until tea the Oval will be held to be within

HEADMASTER'S ROOM, MARITZBURG COLLEGE.

bounds. Any boy requiring to visit the City on special grounds must apply at the times specified to the Headmaster, from whom alone leave may be obtained.

13. No game may be played except on the ground bounded by the main approach and the path leading from the Park to the College. Due care must be taken not to damage trees nor obstruct pathways.

14. On Sundays every boy must attend the place of worship specified by his parents or guardian, and College hats only may be worn. Leave may be obtained to spend the interval between the morning and evening services with any duly accredited friend.

15. Weekly boarders must prepare Monday's lessons on Friday evening, and return to the College before 9 a.m. on Monday.

COLLEGE ATHLETES.

16. Failure on the part of pianoforte pupils to practice at the times appointed will entail severe punishment.

17. All purchases, not being cash transactions, must first be sanctioned by the College authorities.

18. All cases of sickness must be at once reported to the Matron or Headmaster, either by the patient in person or by the Prefect of his Dormitory, if the patient is unable to do so.

Scale of fees :—Upper School, £1 a month ; Lower School, 10s. a month ; Boarding Fee, £4 4s. a month ; Medical Dues, 1s. a month

No " extras " except for necessary text-books.

Total cost for boarding pupil for ten school months of year :—Upper School, £52 10s. ; Lower School, £47 10s.

These fees are payable quarterly in advance :—On 1st February, 15th April, 1st August, and 15th October.

A scheme is at present on foot to utilise the extension of the College lands for Masters' residences, while a new wing is now being added to the main building. This latter addition will provide a hall 75 feet long and 40 feet wide, with an oak-groined roof and cathedral windows, which will be fitted up as a gymnasium and general meeting hall.

From the preceding details, together with the illustrations accompanying them, a fair idea of the status and scope of the Maritzburg College may be gleaned.

An important point which should not be overlooked in dealing with any institution whose misson it is to mould and build up the unformed minds of the rising generation, is that of association and environment. The stately building, the well-regulated and cleanly lives which the boys are required to lead, the association with cultured and gifted mentors, must have the effect of thoroughly impregnating the boys' beings with all that is pure and noble, and of fitting them to discharge in their future lives the duties which may fall to their lot with dignity and ability.

The Maritzburg College, although, like the rest of the Colony, of distinctly modern origin, has already made a record in the lives and deaths of many of its pupils which constitutes a noble history, of which the present collegians have every reason to be proud. The tablet already mentioned as being placed in the entrance hall of the College, was unveiled on the 28th April, 1882, in the old High

School by His Excellency Sir Henry Bulwer, K.C.M.G., etc., the then Governor of the Colony, Sir John Akerman, K.C.M.G., the Mayor of Maritzburg, and many other officials being present.

As the event was one of considerable importance to the school and interest to the City, we cannot do better than place the address to the Governor and subsequent speeches on permanent record, in order that they may serve as an incentive to future generations, not only of College pupils, but of rising colonists generally.

The following is the Address :—

To His Excellency Sir Henry Ernest Bulwer, K.C.M.G., &c., &c.

MAY IT PLEASE YOUR EXCELLENCY—

We, the undersigned, on behalf of former pupils and Masters past and present of the Pietermaritzburg High School, with great pleasure meet Your Excellency on this occasion, knowing as we do your deep sympathy with those who suffered by the sad event we this day piously commemorate, and the great interest which Your Excellency has ever manifested in that which is educative in tendency, as we trust the simple memorial which we have erected and these proceedings will be.

The desire to perpetuate the memory of their fallen fellow-scholars originated among some old High School boys about two years ago, and with such cordiality was the idea responded to, that, besides realising the original intention of erecting a monument, they are instituting an annual memorial prize in connection therewith

It is the hope of the Memorial Committee that the constant contemplation of this tablet will engender in the minds of the boys who may be here in the future a desire to follow the example of the honoured dead in their unostentatious performance of duty, and that the competition for the Memorial Prize, as one of more than merely intrinsic value, may foster a healthy spirit of emulation and tend to promote the cause of education in the school.

The founders desire that the ceremony of to-day may teach the lesson of simple and unquestioning obedience to duty, and of sacrifice of self, for country and the common weal, and that the acts of the brave departed may bring forth in other boys the fruits of heroic lives and evoke a filial interest in the school whose career is now indelibly identified with the history of the Colony. They would fain hope that this memorial tablet will tend to create among the pupils a desire to do credit to their Alma Mater, and that they may feel that their characters are closely bound up with that of the school, so that it may ever be an honour to have been connected with the High School of Pietermaritzburg.

With these aspirations we now, on behalf of the subscribers, request that Your Excellency will be pleased to unveil the Memorial Tablet which we have been privileged to erect within these walls.

And we have the honour to be,

Your Excellency's obedient servants,

ROBERT D. CLARK, Chairman.
C. H. PEARSE, Honorary Secretary.
High School Memorial Committee.

Mr. Clark, Headmaster of the High School, and Chairman of the Memorial Committee, in presenting His Excellency with the Address, said :—

"In handing this Address to Your Excellency, and previous to requesting you to be pleased to unveil this tablet, I may be permitted to say that I count it a most felicitous concurrence that this, the last act of the programme entrusted to us as a Committee, should fall to be performed by one who can say, as you can, in reference to the historical events which have led to the proceedings of to-day—

> 'Quæque ipse miserrima vidi
> Et quorum pars magna fui.'

It is not for me, in Your Excellency's presence, to dwell on the part you played in these events with such honour to yourself and such benefit to the Colony ; but I cannot help remarking that fortune has, with eminent fitness, arranged that this monument should be unveiled by one who is the foster-father of this institution as at present constituted, and who steered the Colony wisely and well through a period of her history when its need was the sorest. Since Your Excellency last stood within these walls we have as a community lost another very palpable instalment of the proverbial happiness of the people that has no history. Political and social elements have been moving on remorselessly to their natural issues, and this institution being, as I trust it is, in vital connection with the community, has been moving and growing likewise While deeply deploring, in common with all here, the sad events which have led to our meeting now, I cannot but regard this ceremony as a conspicuous landmark in the history of the school. The past boys of to-day are, as it were, joining hands with the present pupils over the graves of the heroic youths whose names, recorded on this tablet, will live in the history of the institution ; and the bright torch lit by these brave lads no High School boy will ever willingly let go out. This monument, and all that it implies, I regard as one of the most potent factors now available for moulding the character of the school, although its action may, and indeed must, be subtle and impalpable We have no lack of youthful talent in our community, and we have a fair share of material prosperity, but these cannot compare in ethical value with the spirit of the storied marble on this wall which will perennially bring to a focus for us the lesson of the discipline of pain, and the bracing influence of difficulties, unflinchingly faced, and overcome even in death. The martyr's blood has been called the seed of the Church, and the patriot's is the best seed of a Constitution. From this day we take a new departure as a school, because we can point with pride to an instalment of our history recorded in the language of the conquerors of the ancient world, the study of which in the school makes us at one with the old academies of the Mother Country. In all I have said I fear I have been speaking more from the point of view of a present Master than from that of the Chairman of the Committee of former pupils. They will, I am sure, forgive me for it. I would only say, in conclusion, that if present and future pupils, when they join the ranks of the old boys, show the same filial spirit towards their Alma Mater, and the same loyal attachment to their fellows as the old boys, to whom the erection of this monument has been a labour of love, I shall count it a privilege to grow grey at my post within these walls. I now request Your Excellency to be pleased to unveil the Memorial Tablet." (Applause).

Sir Henry Bulwer in reply, said :—

Mr. Clark and Mr. Pearse, — I have to thank you, and the former pupils of this school, and Masters past and present, for the address which you have just presented to me, and for what you have also said. I have complied with your invitation to be present on this occasion, and your request that I should unveil this memorial, with cordial satisfaction, not only because of the desire that I naturally have to pay respect to the memory of those who are departed, and my regard for the feelings of their relatives and friends, but also because of my sincere sympathy with the objects which you have in erecting this tablet, and in instituting this annual prize to which you have referred. Your object in erecting this tablet is to commemorate the former *alumni* of this school who fell fighting in the service of their country in the Zulu War, or elsewhere in South Africa, so that it may serve as a memorial of simple obedience, of sacrifice of self, and of heroic deaths, and may be held out as a bright example, both now and in the future, to the boys who shall be educated in this school, and that by means of this honourable association an additional link may be given to bind the boys to their school in filial attachment and in filial pride. There can be no question of the influence that an association of this kind is capable of exercising in early life upon an unformed character by the appeal that it makes to the heart and the imagination of youth; and the influence is not the less powerful, because it is often altogether unconscious. Who can say, for instance, how much our British life and our British character owe to what we may call these unconscious influences. In Britain, with its old-world history, with the historic past, speaking as it were from the very walls of abbey, of castle, or of cloister, or from the stone figures or dim religious light of some storied window, associations of this kind abound. They are associations which, whether at school or in one of our ancient universities, or under the shadow of some grand old cathedral, or by the side of some market cross—are ever speaking to the youth of Britain—are ever speaking, century after century, with occult but eloquent force to the hearts of men as the generations come and go. In a new country associations of this kind are necessarily wanting, and it is therefore the more incumbent upon us that we should secure the remembrance of any event, of any deed, of any life that commends

itself to the hearts of men, and can lay just claim to be
handed down to the attention of posterity. The association
which this tablet is designed to hand down is, it appears to me,
of a peculiarly healthy and beneficial character, and not the
less beneficial because of the simple virtues it recalls. In
the address which you have just presented to me, you refer
to the unquestioning obedience, to the unostentatious performance of duty, and to the self-sacrifice which distinguished
the deaths of those whom we are commemorating this day.
And what better lesson can be taught than that of simple
obedience and unostentatious performance of duty. To do
our duty, to do one's duty faithfully and without fear, with
singleness of heart, and with no thought of self, is a motive
which has produced some of the noblest lives. It is this
principle which we are proud to say has governed, and it is
to this day, under God's blessing, governing the lives of
thousands and thousands of English people ; and I trust
that this principle may never be allowed to die out from
amongst us as a people. Those in whose honour we are
assembled to-day did their duty in simple obedience, and
without fear. It was in the performance of their duty, for
they went forth when the war broke out, and it was in the
performance of their duty that they fell, meeting their
deaths—as became Britons--bravely. This tablet, then,
which records their fate, is a record also of their virtue.
Those whose names are inscribed on it were once, and not
many years ago, pupils at this school. They were then
strong in youth, strong in hope, and as full of the promise of
life as any of those whom I see before me. The thread of
life with them was cut long before its natural time, and they
are gone. But this tablet, which is erected to their memory,
being a record of lives given up in the service of their
country with unquestioning obedience, being a record of
men who, in the performance of their duty, were faithful

unto death, is placed here in the trust that it will not speak in vain to the generations of schoolboys who may sit in their places, but that it may be the means of helping to noble thoughts, and to the formation of manly, brave, and duty-loving lives.

His Excellency at this stage unveiled the tablet, which bears the following inscription :—

"DULCE ET DECORUM EST PRO PATRIA MORI."
IN PIAM MEMORIAM
HUJUS SCHOLÆ ALUMNORUM
QUI UT OLIM PUERI INTER STUDIA LUDOSQUE
Æ MULI FUERANT
SIC JUVENES CONTRA BARBAROS PRO ARIS ET FOCIS
ALIUS ALIO FORTIUS
PUGNANTES
MORTEM OPPETIVERUNT
HOC MONUMENTUM
ICTI DESIDERIO CONDISCIPULI MAGISTRIQUE
HIC ERIGENDUM CURAVERUNT.
R. H. ERSKINE, N.C., APUD "BUSHMAN'S PASS,"
PRID: NON: NOV., MDCCCLXXIII.

J. P. ARCHBELL. N.N.C.
J. A. BLAIKIE, N.C.
H. W. DAVIS, N.C.
F. G. DOYLE, L.H.
F. J. D. SCOTT, N.C.
G. T. MACLEROY, N.C.
G. J. P. SHEPSTONE, N.N.C.
} APUD "ISANDHLWANA,"
XI. KAL. FEB.,
MDCCCLXXIX.

C. A. POTTER, W.N.C., APUD "HLOBANE," V. KAL.
APRIL, MDCCCLXXIX.
J. FERREIRA, C.D., APUD "KAMBULA," IV. KAL.
APRIL, MDCCCLXXIX.
C. MEARS, APUD "SECOCOENI," FINES IV. KAL.
DEC., MDCCCLXXIX.

PIETERMARITZBURGH, MENSE JANUARIO,
MDCCCLXXXII.

We may add that the inscription was written by Mr. Clark, Headmaster of the School, and the tablet has been erected by Messrs. Jesse Smith & Son.

The following brief sketch of the lives of those referred to in the foregoing function will be of interest:—

ROBERT HENRY ERSKINE,

son of the Honourable Major Erskine, for many years Colonial Secretary of the Colony of Natal, was born in India on the 26th July, 1846. He was one of the foundation boys

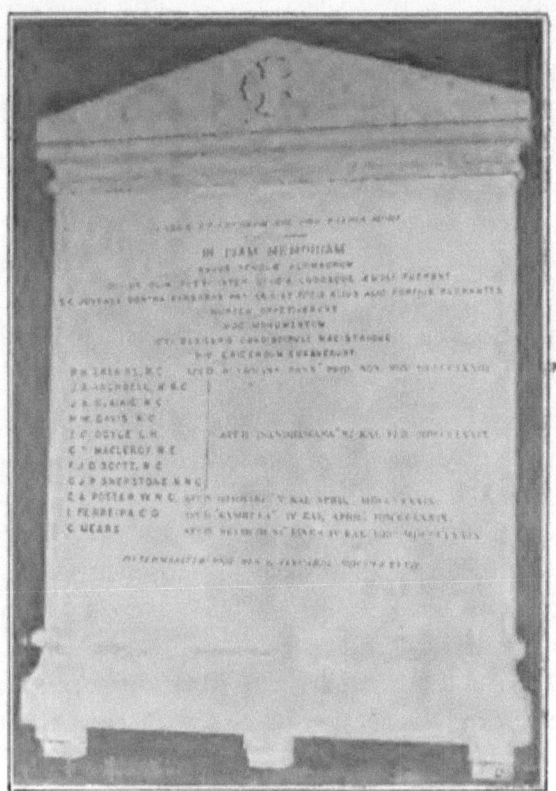

MEMORIAM TABLET, MARITZBURG COLLEGE.

of the High School, Pietermaritzburg, where he won for himself the esteem of his fellow-scholars. After leaving school, he became Private Secretary to His Excellency R. W. Keate, Esq., Lieutenant-Governor of the Colony, and was subsequently admitted as an Advocate of the Supreme

Court. He joined the Natal Carbineers, in which corps he served as a trooper, meeting his death on the 4th November, 1873, at the age of 27, at Bushman's Pass, when one wing of that corp was exposed to the fire of the escaping Amahlubi, in what is known as the Langalibalele expedition.

JAMES PHILIP ARCHBELL

was born on the 13th October, 1853, at Pietermaritzburg. He studied at the High School during the years 1863 and 1864, and twice obtained the Good-Fellowship Prize by the vote of his school-fellows. After leaving school, he first became a clerk in Pietermaritzburg, and subsequently engaged in agricultural pursuits. He volunteered as a non-commissioned officer in the Natal Native Contingent, raised for the defence of the Colony during the Zulu war. As Colour-Sergeant of the 1st Native Contingent, he fell at Isandhlwana, 22nd January, 1879.

JAMES ADRIAN BLAIKIE

was born at Aberdeen, Scotland, on 2nd March, 1859. He entered the High School, June, 1869, remaining until December, 1872, when he had risen to a high position in the school. He then went to Fettes' College, Edinburgh. Returning again to the Colony, he first entered the Civil Service, and then a solicitor's office, where he was long remembered for his remarkable intelligence. During this time he joined the Natal Carbineers as a trooper, and lost his life on 22nd January, 1879, on the field of Isandhlwana. His remains were identified as amongst those who fell surrounding their leader.

HARRY WILLIAM DAVIS,

son of Mr. Peter Davis, one of the oldest colonists of Natal, was born at Pietermaritzburg on the 26th November, 1859. He was at the High School for five years, from 1873 to Christmas, 1877. When he left he had attained the position of third in the First Class. He entered a merchant's office in this City, and became a trooper in the Natal Carbineers, falling at Isandhlwana on 22nd January, 1879. With Blaikie, his body was found close to that of the noble Durnford.

THOMAS GERALD DOYLE,

son of Mr. P. Doyle, was born on the 22nd March, 1859, and studied at the High School during 1871 and 1872, when he was in the Second Division. After leaving school he entered a solicitor's office in Pietermaritzburg, and subsequently went to Kokstadt, where he gained a very good name. At a later date he entered the service of the Railway contractors. He became a Conductor in Lonsdale's Horse, and was killed at Isandhlwana on 22nd January, 1879. His body was found by his father near those of Captain Bradstreet, (B.B.G.), Lieutenant Hitchcock, and S. Grant. They had evidently made a stand together, and fallen fighting. Four months later his remains were interred by his father.

GEORGE THOMSON MACLEROY,

son of the late Mr George Macleroy, for many years General Manager of the Natal Bank, was born at Pietermaritzburg on the 7th November, 1856, and entered the High School about the year 1867. He remained at the school for six years, occupying, when he left, a prominent position in the Upper Room. During this period he won for himself many friends, and on more than one occasion was awarded the Good-Fellowship Prize by them. He was greatly esteemed for his kind and genial disposition, and will long be remembered for his wit and humour ; as a caricaturist, also, he was much appreciated. On leaving school he entered into commercial life, and by close attention to duty gave promise of a successful future. Shortly before the Zulu War he joined the Natal Carbineers, and, like so many of his comrades, did not survive the action at Isandhlwana, 22nd January, 1879. At a subsequent date his remains were removed to the City cemetery by his sorrowing parents.

FREDERICK JOHN DURRANT SCOTT,

son of Mr. D. B. Scott, one of the early settlers in the Colony, was born at Pietermaritzburg on the 19th April, 1851. He was a foundation boy of the High School, and continued there until 1866, when he occupied the second place in the school, and then left to finish his education at Godolphin School, Hammersmith. There he not only passed through his curriculum with much credit, but distinguished himself in athletic exercises—in 1868 winning a medal as the best athlete in the school, and in the same year the average bat. In after years he maintained this character, and was ever distinguished for his prowess in sports. Returning to the Colony, he first filled the position of a clerk in a merchant's office, and subsequently became a partner in the firm of Messrs. Mason & Scott. He joined the Natal Carbineers in 1874, and rose to the rank of second Lieutenant. He marched to the front in December, 1878, and was in command on the 22nd January, 1879, when he fell at Isandhlwana by the side of Colonel Durnford. He left behind him the name of a brave Volunteer, esteemed and beloved by his men.

GEORGE JOHN PALMER SHEPSTONE,

son of Sir Theophilus Shepstone, K.C.M.G., was born at Pietermaritzburg on the 11th June, 1849. After studying at the High School, he went to Capetown to finish his education. On his return he successively held the appointments of Secretary to the Chief Justice and Registrar of the Supreme Court, and thereafter was admitted as an Advocate. Subsequently he entered into commercial life, and became a partner of the firm of Messrs. Henderson & Co.

He joined the Natal Native Horse raised at the commencement of the Zulu War, and became Staff Officer of the late Colonel Durnford, with the rank of Captain On the 22nd January, 1879, the Natal Native Horse were hurried up to support the camp at Isandhlwana. No record remains of the circumstances under which he met his death. Of a friendly disposition, and universally popular, he was deeply lamented by a large number of friends and companions.

CHARLES ALFRED POTTER

was born on the Berea, Durban, on the 29th July, 1853, and entered the High School in August, 1864, remaining until June, 1868. He passed through most of the classes of the school, and each year carried off prizes, the last being December, 1867, when he was head boy of the Second Class. The reports of his attendance showed that he valued his privileges, as the records remaining show that he was never late nor absent for the period to which they refer. Genial, kind, and benevolent, he was beloved by all his companions. On leaving school he went into the Transvaal trading with his father, and was also occupied part of his time as a bookkeeper. When the Zulu War commenced he joined Major-General Wood's First Native Contingent, under Major Leet, which followed the General to Kambula. He was Interpreter and Guide to Colonel Rowland's Column, on the Amaswazi border, and was selected on several occasions as special messenger to the Swazi King. He had before been repeatedly employed by the Transvaal Government as confidential messenger to Cetywayo. On the 28th March, 1879, he left Kambula Camp with Major-General Wood, and was amongst the ill-fated on the Hlobane Hill who could not make good their escape. He was on several occasions mentioned in despatches, and was referred to by name by Sir E. Wood in his public speeches on his return to England. Wherever he moved he sustained the character of an upright gentleman, kind and courageous, beloved by his comrades in arms.

IGNATIUS FERREIRA

(familiarly known as Jonkey), son of Mr. Philip Ferreira, a pioneer in the Colony of Natal, was born at Pietermaritzburg on the 8th February, 1850. He was several years at the High School, where he became known as one always to the front in athletic sports and manly exercises. After leaving school he entered the Master of the Supreme Court's Office, remaining there for two years; afterwards he assisted his father in the business of auctioneer. Whilst living in Maritzburg he joined the Natal Carbineers, of which Corps he continued to be a member till he left the City for the Diamond Fields, where he lived several years. On the commencement of the Zulu War he went to the front as a civilian, in the capacity of Contractor's Agent, and there accepted a special temporary appointment, and attached himself to the Commissariat Department. He took part in the gallant defence of Kambula on the 29th March, 1879, when the camp was attacked by the full strength of the Zulu army, and at the close of the day was found amongst the dead.

CHARLES MEARS

was one of the first boys who attended the High School. On leaving he went to live in the Transvaal, and fell in the service of the Republic at the storming of Mathebi's Kop (Secocoeni Campaign) in the year 1878.

The Council of Education, immediately after its formation in 1878, took steps for complying with the law regarding the establishment of two Model Schools in Pietermaritzburg, one for boys and one for girls. These were termed model schools, because it was intended that they should train pupil teachers, and employ only the most modern methods of instruction.

The Pietermaritzburg Boys' Model School is under the charge of Mr. F. G. Richmond, an English certificated master, who was brought out to the Colony by the Education Department 26 years ago.

When the Maritzburg College was built the old High School Building became the Boys' Model School, which has since been considerably enlarged, and has now ample accommodation for the 500 pupils in attendance.

The institution has been a complete success from every point of view.

A new building was erected for the Girls' Model School, and Miss Broome (sister of the late Sir Napier Broome) was brought from England as its first Headmistress. This school also accommodates its full complement of 500 pupils, and has supplied many teachers now at work in all parts of the Colony.

When the Boys' Model School was moved into the old High School Building the rooms vacated were used as a school for girls living in the eastern parts of the town. Miss Jarvis, then first assistant to Miss Broome, was appointed Mistress. When Miss Broome afterwards resigned, Miss Jarvis was promoted to the Headmistress-ship of the Model School, and Miss Beeston, L.L.A., first assistant in the Girls' Model School, Durban, succeeded Miss Jarvis. This institution has also exceeded the utmost expectations of those who were instrumental in getting it established, chief amongst whom was that public-spirited citizen, Mr. J. J. Chapman, of the Town Council.

This gentleman, aided by Mr. Stephen Stranack, the Town Clerk, left no stone unturned to keep the institution not only going, but to retain it in its present position.

The attendance of this school has reached its utmost limit of 450, and steps are now being taken by the Government to have the building enlarged.

All the appliances, furniture, and methods of instruction in the foregoing schools are of the most modern and approved description.

Passing now from Government institutions to others of a private or a semi-private description, we have many other establishments well worthy of mention.

BLENHEIM SCHOOL.

A capital example of a first-class private school is afforded in the establishment known as "Blenheim School,"

BLENHEIM SCHOOL.

conducted by Mr. R. H. Oldfield. This school was opened five years ago, and has had a career of conspicuous success. Mr. Oldfield is a trained certificated teacher, and has had many years' experience in school management. Unlike the Headmasters of the public schools, his hands are unfettered, and he can arrange his curriculum in a manner which his experience has taught him to be more suitable to the capabilities of his pupils. The time of the lower forms is devoted wholly to a thorough grounding in those subjects which are essential to good work in the future—reading, writing, arithmetic, &c., together with elementary Latin, Euclid, and Algebra. The lower forms enter for the Oxford Local Examinations, and the upper for the Cape Matriculation. Great attention is devoted to delicate and backward pupils, and those boys who are destined for a commercial career receive instruction in shorthand, bookkeeping, and type-writing.

The health, comfort, physical training and general requirements of the pupils are carefully provided for, as well as their scholastic training. The school buildings comprise a handsome residence standing in its own spacious grounds, in one of the healthiest suburbs of Maritzburg. The school and class-rooms are detached from the house, and are lofty and well ventilated. The recreation grounds are very extensive, and include cricket and football fields, and a good tennis court. The boys are formed into a cadet corps, and are taught military drill under Government supervision.

The domestic department is under the management of a competent lady matron, who is an experienced nurse, and a thoroughly comfortable home is provided. There are three resident masters, besides visiting masters for various subjects, and each pupil receives individual attention in the course of his studies. Mr. Oldfield gives a long list of references to parents and guardians of past pupils, who can all testify to the excellent results of his educational and moral training.

THE GIRLS' COLLEGIATE SCHOOL.

This important educational establishment is situated near the centre of Burger Street, and was founded in 1878. At present the pupils number 106.

The school is conducted by Miss R. M. Mason, who holds the Certificate in Arts for Women of the Edinburgh University.

There is a highly qualified staff of teachers, including specially trained art and kindergarten mistresses, a mistress of method, and resident music mistresses.

Pupils are prepared for the examinations of the Cape University, for various music and art examinations, and for the Natal Teachers' Certificate.

GIRLS' COLLEGIATE SCHOOL.

The school course includes English, French, Latin, music, mathematics, science, needlework, class-singing, drawing, and physical exercises.

Other subjects, such as German, Dutch, &c., can be taken on special terms.

The school is non-sectarian, and arrangements are made for boarders to attend the church to which their parents belong.

The establishment may be described as a seminary, worked as nearly as possible on the lines of a British high school for girls.

The training and preparation of teachers is an important item in the school course, and ample scope is afforded in this direction by the method of placing the kindergarten and juvenile classes under an experienced mistress, who is assisted in her work by the student teachers.

The school buildings consist of a central hall, fitted up as a gymnasium, with class-rooms adjoining. A commodious and well-lighted art studio, well furnished with casts and models, is provided, while the care which is lavished on every hand proclaims to even the casual observer the fact that it is no longer necessary for girls to leave the City in order to acquire the training, both educational and methodical, which is essential to the future happiness of a British gentlewoman.

The residential department of the school is separated from the class and work-rooms by a long corridor, and there again, health, sanitation, and the utmost care combine to ensure the maximum of comfort and health.

Touching the latter important subject, we learned that no cases of sickness of a serious or contagious description have occurred; in fact, the health record of the school is phenomenal.

Sports are amply provided for in lawn tennis courts and the gymnasium already referred to, while the extensive grounds and gardens (about four acres) afford ample opportunity to the students to enjoy that open air life which is so essential to health. Indeed, no such suitable premises for educational purposes are to be found elsewhere in South Africa.

THANET HOUSE SCHOOL

is conveniently situated at the corner of Longmarket and Chapel Streets, in the premises formerly occupied by the Engineer-in-Chief of the Natal Government Railways and his staff.

The building, which has been enlarged by the addition of two large wings and an upper storey, is lofty, well ventilated, and, from a sanitary point of view, practically perfect.

THANET HOUSE SCHOOL.

There is dormitory accommodation for about 40 residential pupils, whose health and comfort have been studied in every detail.

The school, which was established in 1882, provides a sound and high class education for girls.

The general course of instruction comprises :—Holy Scripture, history, English language and literature, geography, arithmetic, mathematics, natural science, Latin, French, perspective and model freehand drawing, needlework, and drilling.

There is a gymnasium for the younger pupils. Class singing is taught throughout the school. Great care is taken to ensure a good foundation being laid in the elementary forms.

The work of the pupils is tested annually by the delegacy of Oxford Schools Examinations, and girls are also prepared for the Oxford Local Examination, Preliminary, Junior, and Senior ; and for examinations in theory and practice of music, in connection with Trinity College, London, and Cape University.

There is a kindergarten under an experienced mistress, in which boys as well as girls are received.

The hours of attendance for daily pupils are from 8.30 a.m. to 1.30 p.m.

The Lady Principals, Mrs. Edmonds and Miss Maas, are assisted by a large staff of certificated and well qualified teachers, among whom are the following : Piano and singing, Mr. and Mrs. Day, Miss Ethel Gordon, Miss Varley, Mr. Campbell-Rowland, Miss Maude Day, etc. ; violin, Miss Deane ; freehand, perspective, model drawing, Miss Butler, etc.

The building is electric lighted throughout, and the class-rooms, dining-room, etc., are models of spaciousness and comfort.

The following are particulars as to fees : -

PER QUARTER.

Boarders over 12 years of age	10 guineas.
Boarders under 12 years of age...	9 ,,
Weekly boarders	8 ,,
Laundress	1 guinea.
Board during vacation	25s. per week.

DAY PUPILS.

Forms VI. and V. ...	2½ guineas.
Form IV. ...	2 „
Forms III. and II....	£1 15s.
Form I. ...	£1 10s.
Kindergarten from 9 to 1 o'clock	1 guinea.
„ „ 8.30 to 1.30 ...	£1 5s.

EXTRA SUBJECTS.

Pianoforte ...	from £1 10s. to 2½ guineas.
„ Kindergarten	1 guinea.
Violin ...	2 guineas.
Theory of music and harmony ...	7s. 6d.
Singing ...	2 guineas.
German ...	2 „
Drawing and painting ...	2 „
Dancing ...	15s.
Dancing and calisthenics...	1 guinea.

Special terms for two or more sisters.

The school year is divided into four quarters, of ten weeks each, commencing respectively about February 3rd, April 13th, August 3rd, and October 12th.

The fees for each quarter are payable in advance, and a quarter's notice is required previous to the removal of a pupil.

Boarders are allowed to visit friends (with their parents' approval), from Saturday to Monday at the end of each month.

MERCHISTON SCHOOL,

a preparatory day and boarding school for boys, is situated near the head of Prince Alfred Street, overlooking the Park, and presents an imposing frontage to the eastward, embracing a magnificient view of mountain and forest scenery.

The school was established in 1892 by Miss Allan and Miss Agnes Rowe.

It is the endeavour of the Lady Principals and their staff to arouse in their pupils an intelligent interest in, and enthusiasm for, their studies ; and to train them in gentlemanly and honourable habits of thought, speech and action.

The class-rooms have ample accommodation for one hundred pupils, whilst forty is the limit fixed for the number of those in residence.

In addition to the two Principals, a staff of five resident mistresses is attached to the establishment, while visiting mistresses attend for instruction in piano and violin.

The school might well take rank as a Collegiate Institute, for the curriculum includes many branches of education not generally taught in a juvenile boys' school.

MERCHISTON SCHOOL.

The ages of the pupils range from five to fourteen; boarders are received from the age of seven.

The youngest boys are educated on a modified kindergarten system by specially trained mistresses; the elder boys receive instruction in Latin and mathematics, in addition to the ordinary English subjects The highest class prepares every year for the Preliminary Oxford Examination.

We have learned that the boys prepared in this institution take good positions upon entering the more advanced schools of the Colony or Britain.

A spacious cricket field and recreation ground is attached to the premises. Masters attend the school to give instruction in drill, cricket, and swimming, and some of the elder boys belong to the Cadet Corps of the Colony.

Manly sports are encouraged in every way, and it is only justice to Miss Allan and Miss Rowe to say that the spirit which pervades the place is one calculated to foster and develop a spirit of manliness in the boys who are entrusted to their care.

The buildings present the acme of comfort. Every care has been lavished on the ventilation and sanitation of the class-rooms, dormitories, and offices, and above all, system and method are inculcated in every department of life.

The Lady Principals are assisted in the case of the residential pupils by an experienced and competent matron.

It is safe to say that the parent must indeed be hard to please who would hesitate to entrust his son to the care of the two courteous ladies who preside over the establishment.

FUTURE STUDENTS.

CHAPTER XVII.

Sport in the City.—Racing.—Athletics.—Field Sports.

WE are indebted to Mr. George Bull, of the *Witness* staff, for much of the following information.

In Maritzburg, as in most South African towns, sport plays an important part in the life of the community. Most of the manly games and pastimes which find so much favour in the old country, and are now regarded as "national," are keenly followed. Cricket, football, tennis, golf, and polo, each have their exponents, and when the size and population of the town are taken into consideration, it is little short of marvellous that such proficiency should be attained as is actually achieved. To cite an example. During the winter of 1897 a team representing the Corinthians—the most powerful amateur Association football combination in England—visited Maritzburg, and met a team drawn from the local clubs. The visitors had been told on their arrival at the Cape that they would find Natal the South African stronghold of Association football, and this being their first match in the Colony, they naturally made every effort to preserve their unbroken record. The result of the encounter was a victory for the Corinthians by a solitary goal to nothing; and this in face of the fact that the Englishmen were opposing the representatives of a team with a white population equal to that of a moderate-sized English village.

Before the discovery of the Witwatersrand Gold Fields, Maritzburg enjoyed the distinction of being one of the most important racing centres in the country. Of late years, however, matters in connection with the Turf have not been in such a healthy condition as they were in former days. Powerful efforts have been made to revive the "Sport of Kings," and to attract public support, but up to the present it cannot be said that these efforts have met with any great measure of success. Maritzburg is in possession of an admirable racecourse, delightfully situated and capitally equipped, but of late years it has been used solely for Sporting Club, Garrison, and indifferently-supported Turf Club meetings, the racing being almost entirely confined to local candidates, several of whom, however, have at more important gatherings acquitted themselves in a manner which has reflected the greatest credit on their breeders and trainers. The most successful meetings held are those promoted by the City Sporting Club—a flourishing organization, the praiseworthy efforts of which have gone a long way to prevent racing from becoming entirely extinct. The racecourse has passed into the hands of a company, known as the New Grand Stand Company, whose meetings are held under the rules of the Jockey Club of South Africa, affiliation to that body having been decided upon in the hope that Rand owners and others would be induced to support local racing. So far the stakes offered have not proved sufficiently tempting, and past experience has proved that, in face of the public support accorded to the various meetings, it would be idle for the promoters to launch out further.

As regards athletics and field sports, considerable progress has been made in Maritzburg of late years. Cricket and football are both extremely popular, each claiming a large number of devotees. The cricket season extends over a period of eight months—from September to April—and throughout that period, it may truthfully be written, the Park Oval (on which the principal matches are played) is occupied four days in the week. Maritzburg has given to the world more than one cricketer who has proved his right to be included in the front rank. Take, for instance, that brilliant young willow-wielder, Mr. C. O. H. Sewell, who, on being included in the South African team which visited England in 1894, though barely out of his teens, was the only member of the combination to score over 1,000 runs, and had moreover the distinction of heading the batting averages. Since that time he has been a regular member of the Gloucestershire County eleven. In the annual intercolonial contests, Maritzburg has always been able to contribute its quota of representatives to the teams chosen to uphold the Colony's interests, and in the intertown games, played every year, the Capital has held its own with the Port. The introduction of the League system in connection with purely local cricket has had the effect of giving a fillip to the summer pastime, and of popularising the game with the public. Another indication of progress is the effort now being made by the local cricket authorities to secure the services of a professional coach.

A remarkable feature in connection with the history of football in Maritzburg is that whereas in the early days the Rugby game was the most popular, now the "handling" code is practically a dead letter, and interest is confined to the Association game. Efforts have been made to revive the Rugby game, but without success. In Durban the game is quite neglected; in Maritzburg its followers are few. The votaries of the Association game are exceedingly numerous, and the progress of the various cup competitions (both senior and junior) is watched with keen interest. The cup finals, as well as the annual intertown contests, are played alternately in Durban and Maritzburg, the principal struggle being that between the premier clubs of Durban and Maritzburg for possession of the "Greaves" trophy. A fact worthy of notice is that while the majority of intertown matches between the two towns have been drawn, the "Greaves" cup finals have invariably resulted in favour of Durban's representatives. Maritzburg players took a prominent part in securing for Natal in 1896 the gold cup presented to the South African Football Association by Sir

Donald Currie for competition between the various Colonies and States, and also in obtaining for Natal the distinction of having given the Corinthians the hardest game of their tour.

Athletic sports and cycling are so closely connected nowadays that they may be treated as one subject. The progress of athletics in the City has been particularly marked. A few years since, race meetings were conduted on the most primitive lines. Prizes were solicited from local tradesmen, and the public were admitted free. The spectators, no doubt, enjoyed the sport, but the poor competitors very often had to wait a long while for their prizes, which were generally orders on storekeepers for clothing, liquor, photographs, and so forth. All this has been altered. The Maritzburg Athletic Club is now a properly constituted body, affiliated to the South African Amateur Athletic Association, under whose laws all meetings are held. Gate money enables the club to offer valuable prizes for competition, and the contests are of a much higher standard than formerly, and individual performances of a more meritorious character. Maritzburg has for some time now been the stronghold of athleticism in the Colony, and not long ago, at an important meeting held in Durban, the City representatives swept the board, J. L. Ballenden winning the 220 yards championship, and J. H. Moodie obtaining the 100 yards championship. It is questionable whether the Colony has produced two such capable performers on the path since the days of Ted Smith, Brunton, and McCrystal. As regards cycling, Maritzburg has not yet given to the world a Mentjes, a Griebenow, or a Van Heerden, but the fascinating pastime has of late undergone remarkable development, and bids fair to become even more popular. It is only within the past two years that Maritzburg has become possessed of anything that could be likened to a cycling track, and there can be little doubt that it is to this fact that Maritzburg's backwardness, as compared with other centres, is attributable. The City boasts of two cycling clubs—the Speedwell, which has a membership of close on 100, and the Rovers, an off-shoot of the old organisation. Maritzburg, moreover, is the headquarters of the Natal Cyclists Union—a governing body of recent origin, the formation of which has supplied a long-felt want. Race meetings are frequently held, but the present track in the Park will have to be considerably improved, or a new track constructed, before it will be possible to chronicle performances on the "wheel" of more than ordinary merit. Road races are popular, and an annual fixture is an intertown race betwen Durban and Maritzburg club representatives.

Golf, lawn tennis, and polo also have their devotees, but naturally do not enjoy the same measure of popularity as the pastimes which have been dealt with.

CHAPTER XVIII.

Conclusion.—A Word Picture.—The Opening of the First Parliament under the new Constitution.—The Past and Present.—Her Majesty's Jubilee.—Poem.—The Last Scene.

IN the preceding pages, we venture to think, the reader will find a fairly complete description of the African City as it stands to-day. It but remains to resume the allegory of a drama, and raise the curtain for the last time on a stage which has been the scene of so many heroic events and so much manful endeavour.

Last time the actors appeared was on the occasion of the opening of the first Parliament in Natal.

The time of this one is the 20th June, 1893, and the scene no longer circles around the humble structure previously mentioned.

The full blaze of the noonday sun is flooding the City. The streets are thronged with well-dressed multitudes, and but few evidences remain of the primitive town which has been so often pictured.

No lumbering caravan finds room in the busy thoroughfares. Open carriages, bearing fair dames, who would faint in horror to hear the stories the very stones of the street might tell, roll luxuriously past, while horsemen and horses well clad and groomed are to be seen on every hand. Here and there amongst the equestrians and on the pavements are many of the sons and daughters of the rugged pioneers who first set their mark on the virgin soil where the City now stands. There amongst the Councillors, with figure still erect, is one of the veritable voortrekkers himself, sturdy and strong, with his granchildren clustered around him. Notwithstanding his impassive expression, it is safe to say, as his eye ranges over the brilliant scene, that his mind casts back to those other days when, instead of the tender hand of a prattling child, he grasped his ready rifle, and in the name of God and progress held his life as naught in the face of threatening hosts, and so he rests in the eventide of his life, and the world rolls on.

The clock in the stately tower high over head chimes the quarter before noon. But fifteen minutes of the old order remain ; but fifteen minutes, and a new epoch dawns, when Natal the wilderness, the theatre of war, the African Republic, the province of the Cape and the Crown Colony, will pass out from the sheltering wings of the Motherland, and consummate the dreams of her pioneers by becoming an independent, self-governing State.

A new Parliament is about to be opened, and a new life begun.

Hark, there is a stir in the streets ! A regiment of British cavalry wheels into view, a guard of honour of

British infantry forms up, the clock chimes the hour of noon, and the answering guns from Fort Napier boom out a farewell to the passing, and a welcome to the coming, order.

One more epoch scene remains to be depicted before the finale.

In common with the whole of the British Empire, the citizens of Maritzburg sought to commemorate in fitting fashion the celebration of the Sixtieth Year of Her Most Gracious Majesty's reign.

JUBILEE PROCESSION IN MARITZBURG.

Once more the town is decked with bunting. The streets are bowered with palm leaves, and the crash of martial music fills the air.

No mere lip homage stirs the multitudes that throng the sidewalks; processions, miles long, fill the streets. The whole stage is covered with the banners of peace. There march the trades' processions, each with its symbol held aloft. There follow the friendly societies, with the emblems of their craft, then a host of others, with fluttering banners and sashes. The very streets are paved with silk. Gold emblazonments shimmer in the sun, a British General leads the procession of joy, while children by the thousand, ten times told, lend hope and promise of the future in a ceremony that consecrates the past. "God Save the Queen" is echoed along the streets, "God save and spare her long." Hark to the swelling chant, 'tis Afric's greeting to "Victoria":

> "Wake! land whose fetters fell at England's bidding,
> Wake! hearts that bled beneath grim slavery's yoke.
> Join hands ye tribes and greet the mighty ruler,
> Who willed your freedom, and your thraldom broke.
>
> From darksome forest glades, from sun-swept rivers,
> From town and village, from hill and vale,
> Comes forth the gladsome cheer, 'Victoria-Empress
> Our Queen, our Mother, God be with thee.
>   Hail! hail! Empress-Queen.'
>
> Lift up your hands, ye tribes and far-off nations,
> Lift up your hands to highest Heaven and pray,
> That God may save and bless our well-beloved,
> And guard her from all peril day by day.
>
> A world-wide Empire, yea, a band of Empires
> In chorus blends its many millioned voice,
> And clasping hands o'er Continents and Oceans,
> Rings out the royal cheer, Rejoice, Rejoice.
>
> A million sabres gird thy throne and person,
> A million champions guard thee day and night,
> Yet over all thy nation's deep-set homage,
> Is thy best buckler, and thy truest might.
>
> Thy voice, thy name, thy flag, these are our glories,
> Our lives, our all, are consecrate to thee,
> For thou hast taught us by thy life's example
> How to be faithful, noble, fearless, free.
>
> From darksome forest glades, from sun-swept rivers,
> From town and village, from hill and vale,
> Comes forth the gladsome cheer, 'Victoria-Empress
> Our Queen, our Mother, God be with thee.
>   Hail! hail! Empress-Queen.'"

and so the procession blends into the past, bearing with it far and wide throughout the State that keynote of loyalty which will yet, in the unwritten future, constitute the

African City still more and more one of the impregnable bulwarks of Britain.

Again the scene is changed. This time the peaceful light of stars illuminates it, sweet strains of music fill the air ; of a truth, the seed sown in the early days has brought forth abundantly. For from the very wilderness has risen a centre of modern culture, wherein the ancient lore of Greece and Rome is taught, where the gospel of peace is preached, where prosperity, begotten of industry prevails, and where above all, deep-rooted as the love of life, is the loyalty of the citizens to the Imperial flag of Britain.

So we close the page, for the story of an African City is told.

Personal Notes.

IN a work dealing with the affairs of a City, its immediate rulers naturally claim some attention at the hands of the historian. The Chief Magistrate of the City, Mr. G. J. Macfarlane, was born in Maritzburg in 1855, and was educated at the High School in the City. He is the son of the late Mr. John Macfarlane, who, for over 20 years, was Resident Magistrate in Weenen County, and nephew of the late Mr. Walter Macfarlane, who held the high office of Speaker of the Legislative Council for over 20 years. The present Mayor, who holds the rank of Major in the Natal Carbineers, served with distinction in the Zulu War. He first entered the Town Council in 1896.

William Ebrington Bale, J.P., member for Ward 1, who was elected Mayor of Maritzburg in 1890, and again in 1893, first joined the Council in 1857.

Thomas Wilson Woodhouse, J.P., Deputy Mayor, member for Ward 6, was elected Mayor of Maritzburg in 1897, and first joined the Council in 1892.

Philip Francis Payn, J.P., member for Ward 5, was elected Mayor of Maritzburg in 1896, and first joined the Council in 1889. He is the Chairman of the Police, &c., Committee.

Charles Goodman Levy, J.P., member for Ward 4, was elected Mayor of Maritzburg in 1895. He has represented this Ward since 1890

John Jex Chapman, J.P., member for Ward 7, was elected Mayor of Maritzburg in 1886, and again for the two following years. He has represented this Ward since 1883.

Richard Mason, J.P., member for Ward 8, was elected Mayor of Maritzburg in 1891, and again for the following year. He first joined the Council 1881.

Thomas Raymond, member for Ward 2, first joined the Council in 1892.

William Samuel Crart, member for Ward 4, first joined the Council in 1895.

William Herbert Buchanan, member for Ward 6, first joined the Council in 1895.

Benjamin Swete Kelly, member for Ward 8, first joined the Council in 1889.

William John O'Brien, member for Ward 5, is the Chairman of the Finance, &c., Committee, and first joined the Council in 1897.

Benjamin Ireland, member for Ward 2, first joined the Council in 1894.

Sowersby Joseph Mason, member for Ward 7, first joined the Council in 1895.

Richard Francis Morcom, member for Ward 3, first joined the Council in 1896, and is Chairman of the Works and Town Hall Restoration Committees.

Clifford Walmslee Barlee Scott, member for Ward 3, first joined the Council in 1895, and is the Chairman of the Fire Brigade Formation Committee.

D. F. Forsyth, B.A., A.S.A.A., joined Corporation Service in June, 1882, and has held appointment of Borough Accountant since 1893.

S. Stranack, J.P., is the present Town Clerk of Maritzburg, and has held that appointment since 1883.

MEMBERS FOR THE CITY.

Hon. Col. HIME, C.M.G., M.L.A.
(Minister of Lands & Works).

Hon. H BALE, Q.C., M.L.A.
(Attorney-General).

Mr. W. B. MORCOM Q.C., M.L.A.

Mr. F. S. TATHAM, M.L.A.

The late J. D. Holliday.

The late Jas. Raw.

Late Mr. E. Buchanan, J.P.

J. Welch (Post Contractor).

The Story of an African City.

Mr. D. Hunter, C.M.G.
(General Manager of Railways).

Mr. R. H. Mason.

Mr. R. Topham.

PART III.

BUSINESS REVIEW.

Early Trade—Mr. Barter's Book—The Ubiquitous Auctioneer—Boer Vernuckers—Trade Established—Messrs. Mowat & Still—Messrs Brady & Wyles—Messrs. Collins & Munro—Mr. J. Hughes—Mr Henry Collins—Messrs. Jesse Smith & Son—Messrs. David Whitelaw &¦ Son—Messrs. Merryweather & Sons—Messrs. R. McAlister & Sons—Mr. John Hardy—Mr. D. Nicolson—Messrs. Turner & Company—Mr. Thomas Hannah—Mr. Robert Fuller—Messrs. P. Henwood, Son, Soutter & Company—Messrs. Clifford and Smith—Messrs. Mason & Broadbent—Messrs. Taylor & Fowler—Mr. J. C. Baumann—Imperial Hotel—List of Mayors of Pietermaritzburg—Cab Stands and Cab Fares—Jinricksha Stands and Fares.

IN the preceding chapters it has been the earnest endeavour of the author, to set forth with pen and camera the undoubted claims to consideration which the City possesses to be regarded as an important educational centre.

Its progress has been pourtrayed in nearly every aspect from the earliest times, when it was still a portion of the wilderness, to its present condition as a Corporate City, the capital of an important Colony, replete with those institutions which are rendered necessary by the present high state of civilisation, and rapidly becoming widely popular as a health and pleasure resort.

There is one aspect, however, which must yet be dealt with, if this work is to fulfil its important mission of acquainting the outside world with the City and its life, as they stand at the present moment.

It would be unnecessarily wearisome to burden these pages with masses of trade statistics which would merely tend to adduce proof of a progress which already has been shown. At the same time, it would be manifestly wrong to bring the book to a conclusion without making a more than passing mention of that backbone of prosperity—trade. The wonderful change which has taken place in the commercial life of Maritzburg, and those who are engaged in it, would perhaps be the first matter to attract the attention of a stranger.

Forty years ago the stores of Maritzburg were for the most part sort of curiosity shops, where the purchaser might obtain anything from a needle to an anchor. Nothing was "too hot or too heavy," so to speak, for the enterprising dealer.

In his charming, but, alas, too rare volume, "The Dorp and the Veld," Charles Barter, Esq., B.C.L., Natal's veteran Magistrate, and deeply revered friend, has given a series of vivid word pictures, pourtraying in his own happy vein the trading life of Maritzburg, at which the established and prosperous merchant of the present day would probably smile

It appears that the auctioneer was the universal friend of buyer and seller alike, while the storekeeper contented himself with the accumulations of rattle traps and odds and ends, which he picked up during his Saturday lounge on the auction marts. The aforesaid storekeeper oftentimes combined in himself the various functions of merchant, local preacher, horse breaker, pawnbroker, and lawyer. All were fish that came to his net, and be it spoken to his credit, he, as a rule, used his unlimited power with marked consideration.

The trade in those days was spasmodic, depending for the most part on the wool, ivory, and hides which the Boers and others periodically brought to market. Amusing episodes were not wanting in the traffic which ensued; for those who brought their wares for sale in exchange for such commodities as calico, coffee, fustian, and lead were by no means paragons of honesty and truth, The result was, the storekeeper was put on his metal, in order to protect himself. A class of middleman sprung up, who speadily earned for himself the title of "Boer-vernucker," whose exalted mission it was to save each contracting party from the other, and, oftentimes by sharp practice, feather his own nest, to the serious disadvantage of both sellers and buyers.

This state of affairs continued for some time, until by a natural process, it remedied itself. There are, however, still in Maritzburg some lingering representatives of the class, who look back on the good old days with vain regret.

The new era requires no special description further than to say that the various branches of trade have settled themselves into their own grooves, and the town, from a business point of view, has assumed the characteristics of any other trading centre, where competition exists. Nowadays the ivory and gold trader has passed away to make room for those who cater for modern necessities. Amongst these, and as a fair indication of the progress which the African City has achieved, is the firm of Messrs. Mowat & Still, whose business was first founded in Natal by Mr. William Mowat, as a contractor on the N.G.R. in 1882, where he carried out contracts on the extension of the main line between Maritzburg and Ladysmith.

In 1884 Mr. Mowat settled in Estcourt as a builder and contractor, where he erected all the handsome stone edifices which now lend dignity to that town. Continuing his work on the railway, he carried out a part of the Ladysmith to Elands Laagte Section, which was granted by the Government for the purpose of bringing down coal from the mines. This section was hardly finished before we find him on the Biggarsberg section, and after having finished this contract he constructed the station at the Biggarsberg, and then carried out the works on Section 1 of the Harrismith extension. Later on he carried out to general satisfaction the famous No. 9 Section, which brought the railway line beyond Van Reenen's Pass into the Orange Free State, where he constructed the Harrismith terminus.

At this period the partnership between Mr. Mowat and Mr. Still commenced. The first work of the new firm was the erection of that beautiful structure, the Dutch Reformed Church, at Harrismith, which is an ornament and credit to church architecture in South Africa.

In 1893 and 1894 they built the Apies River Bridge (costing £15,000), now known as the Lion Bridge, in the Transvaal. In 1895, the firm constructed two bridges over the "De Kaap River" for the Netherlands Railway, one of which is known as Avoca Bridge, and the other as "Joe's Luck Bridge."

In 1896 the firm became associated with Maritzburg, where they established an important business as general contractors, undertaking and carrying out contracts with the City Corporation, the Natal Agricultural Department, etc. These works include the first section of the underground drains, and the construction of the present fine Electric Power Station. Amongst the number of houses in the City they have built must be mentioned the palatial residence of F. S. Tatham, Esq., M.L.A. They also designed and built the two double-storey villas known as "Jubilee Villas," which are an ornament to the upper part of Longmarket Street, as well as many other small residences.

In order to move with the times, Messrs. Mowat & Still have now added to their business an extensive Electrical Engineering Department, and are prepared to tender for and immediately carry out electrical works of any magnitude, either for lighting towns, mines, mills, collieries, country residences as well as power transmission. The firm is also prepared to undertake the connection of dwelling houses and shops with the Town Electrical Supply Mains in accordance with the latest English and American practice, and in order to keep fully abreast with the times they have attached to the firm, as Electrical Manager and Engineer, Mr. Oswald R. Swete, A.M.I.E.E. (London), M.S.E.E. (South Africa), whose office is at 108, Church Street, where an elaborate stock of fittings may be inspected.

Messrs. Brady & Wyles and Messrs. Collins & Munro are two other firms who are fully entitled to special mention in connection with the modern progress of the town.

The former firm, Messrs. Brady & Wyles, have an establishment in Church Street, where they commenced business in 1896.

With commendable enterprise they have launched out in a manner which proves that they possess a fully justified faith in the future growth of the "African City" and Colony where they have established themselves. The firm is in a position at the present moment to supply and instal electric power and light plants anywhere throughout Natal, while constant consignments of the latest inventions and artistic adaptations of electric appliances to almost every imaginable use are regularly added to their stock. The firm is capable of carrying out to a satisfactory issue any work connected with the department of industry with which it is connected.

Mr. William B. Brady was previously asociated with an eminent firm in Newcastle-on-Tyne, where he gained a wide and varied experience which enabled him and his partner, Mr. F. Camp Wyles, who was at one time on the Corporation Electrical Staff, to effect works which tend to bring the City of Maritzburg well into line with many much older cities.

To anyone contemplating the installation of electric light or power plants, a visit to the office and showroom of the firm, which is situated in the very heart of the City, at 192, Church Street, will be time well spent, for the stock of fittings and appliances constitute in themselves an exhibition which is full of interest ; for it not only indicates the scientific advancement of the period, but the fact that though one may reside in this far out African City, it does not follow that the height of modern comfort and luxury may not be fully enjoyed, in as far, at any rate, as the practical application of this century's most wonderful invention extends.

The principal business places in this City have been installed by this firm, two of which include the erection of complete private plant with accumulators. They are also contractors to Natal Government.

Messrs. Collins & Munro, whose establishment is situated in Pietermaritz Street, are a firm which in every way serve as an indication of the wonderful progress which within recent years has been made by Maritzburg. Not only does the establishment of enterprises such as theirs serve to place Maritzburg high on the list of African centres, but it tends further to demonstrate that the people of the City are fully alive to the scientific advantages which this firm can place at their disposal.

Messrs. Collins & Munro are now fully recognised as one of the rising business institutions of the place. As general engineers and machinists, they undoubtedly rank high, but it is more with their electrical department that this chapter is concerned. A walk through their showrooms is quite equal to a visit to an electric exhibition. Novelties, artistic and useful, of every description are to be seen, from the delicately-tinted magic bell of frosted glass, which seems to float in the air like a tiny star, through every grade of shape, form and colour, to huge globes and shades of crystal. Appliances for the utilisation of electric energy, based on latest advances, are to be seen on every hand, and the firm can undertake works in connection with the installation of electric plant for power or lighting purposes on any scale.

Their stock, to which constant additions are being made, has necessitated the securing of a show window in Church Street, in addition to their Pietermaritz Street premises, where a magnificent display, well worthy of a much older-established firm and city, may be inspected.

The prosperity which a firm such as that of Messrs. Collins & Munro has secured may well serve, to the mind of a close observer, as a marked indication of the stage of progress to which the City has now attained.

We have omitted to mention in the previous paragraphs a leading speciality of the firm, which it is safe to say will come as a pleasant revelation to those inclined to avail themselves of electricity for decorative purposes.

Messrs. Collins & Munro have made a special feature of the illumination of ball, concert, and supper rooms, with art silk shade effects. Piano lamp shades, with the same material and bouquets gemmed with electrical lights, are also among the specialties of the firm.

Having glanced briefly at those advanced business institutions which may be regarded in a certain degree as associated with the scientific development of the City, we come now in the course of our business review to those firms that devote their energies more directly to the manufacturing and furnishing departments of trade.

The first amongst these to attract one's attention is Mr. J. Hughes, who is entitled to mention here, in view of the fact that he has more particularly devoted himself to the manufacture of high class and artistic furniture from Colonial timber.

Mr. Henry Collins, as a builder and art decorator, takes high rank, and does an extensive business.

Many others might be mentioned did space permit. We cannot, however, close these remarks without making reference to that veteran firm, Messrs. Jesse Smith & Son, whose magnificient Colonial Office Buildings will stand as a permanent monument to their honour.

Passing from this phase of Maritzburg's progress, attention is next claimed by the industrial firms that work in wood and iron. Of these there are several, principal amongst them being the establishments of Messrs. David Whitelaw & Son and Merryweather & Sons.

The former firm, Messrs. David Whitelaw & Son, is one which may truly be regarded as a landmark in the City. Its place of business, which occupies the greater part of an erf in Commercial Road, for very many years has formed a centre of attraction and trade, when the surrounding parts of the City were yet in primitive garb.

What a ship-building firm is to a seaport, Messrs David Whitelaw & Son are to Maritzburg. From the huge trek-wagon, fitted to battle with the roadless wilds, to the fragile phaeton, which whirls along the modern street, this firm produces from rough-hewn logs, finished and complete, the structures which are necessary to every phase of active life.

A walk through their premises where are stored, ready for emergency, vast quantities of all the necessary ironwork used in the construction of the innumerable varieties of vehicle which the firm manufactures, on through the machine department, where mighty engines of applied human ingenuity rough hew, carve and fashion the wood and iron which are destined in the next workshop to take symmetrical shape and form, is an object lesson in manufacturing industry.

Veritable forests of timber are here stored ready for use, while busy hands are plying their skill in cleaving and turning, planing and modelling the raw material into the finished article.

The skeleton forms of trolleys and carts, wagons and carriages steadily take shape here, and then pass on to the painting department whence they emerge complete and ready, as many of them do, to be entrained for Johannesburg, where the firm for some considerable time now has an important branch of business.

To detail the various departments, which are presided over by Mr. James Whitelaw, who has succeeded his late father in the business, is unnecessary, but it would be unjust to pass on to others without paying a hearty tribute to the enterprise of a firm which has borne its full share in the establishment and advancement of the City of Pietermaritzburg.

Messrs. J. Merryweather & Son, coachbuilders, wagonmakers, and general workers in wood and iron, are as a firm justly entitled to special mention as one of the pioneer institutions of the City.

Arriving here in 1850, the senior partner, subsequently aided by his sons, and joined in 1876 by Mr. J. S. Mason, has steadily prospered with the town, and can now claim to conduct one of the most extensive and successful establishments of its kind in South Africa.

The office of the firm is a commodious structure facing Church Street, while the workshops, which lie behind it, are thoroughly supplied with the latest inventions in labour-saving machinery.

Entering the works from Boshoff Street side, one is confronted with piles of balks of seasoned and valuable timbers, cut, for the most part, from the forests of Natal.

Passing into the workshop, the ear is greeted with the hoarse roaring of steam saws of every variety. In whirling clouds the sawdust flies from the wood, leaving it a spoke, a felloe, or what not.

Boring machines, steam planes, mighty lathes, and tennoning machines buzz and hiss until the mind moves in sympathy with the electric hurry of the century of steam power and science.

Here a powerful engine, with one crush of its mammoth jaws, severs bands of steel and perforates them wherever desired; there silently working, apparently with human intelligence, are patent saw sharpening machines, plane iron setters, and drills.

Next door, in a spacious shop, nine forge fires light up the smoke laden air, while the brawny knights of the hammer "fashion the glowing iron and mould it to their will."

Leaving this room, a wonderful machine is encountered, which at first sight suggests thoughts of the Spanish Inquisition; but there is no fear, it is merely a patent cold-iron-trye-shrinking machine of the very latest pattern, such as are in use at Woolwich and elsewhere throughout Great Britain. Crossing the street to another department, and passing *en route* the dismembered limbs of countless vehicles, the finishing and painting department is encountered, where, ready for their journeys, stand the great trek-wagons, waiting but the order to start like "ships of the desert" to the far-off lands of the Matabele and Mashona. Although the train and cab have supplanted them in the streets of the "African City," those who dwell in the wilds still fall back for them upon the mother town in their necessity.

"Industry and enterprise" is the motto of Messrs. Merryweather & Sons, and well indeed have they upheld it, by the creation and maintenance of an establishment which does honour alike to the firm and the City.

Messrs. R. McAlister & Sons, builders and contractors, of Club Street, Maritzburg, is one of the oldest-established firms in their line in Maritzburg, having commenced business in 1873.

It is from about this date that an improved style of architecture was required in the City, and with characteristic thoroughness Mr. McAlister, afterwards assisted by his sons, supplied the want.

It would take more space than we have at our disposal to enumerate the many fine buildings with which the firm has beautified Maritzburg.

While not professing to be "cheap" builders, the work produced by the firm speaks for itself, and those who place orders with it can confidently rely on stability, combined with elegance ; as witness the Nigel Offices and most of the prominent private residences of the City, such as those of Mr. R. F. Morcom, Mr. Geo. Barter, Mr. Mead, Mr. W. J. O'Brien, Mrs. Thresh, Mr. James Woodhouse, Mr. A. M. Anderson.

The Natal Brewery Buildings were also erected by the firm, which has also carried out all the War Department works at Fort Napier since 1890.

The firm is also prepared to import goods, &c., for the building trade, having by reason of its own extensive operations acquired considerable experience in the selection and purchase of building requisites.

It has been said that Great Britain's colonising success is due, in a great measure, to the efforts and enterprise of her pioneering sons. The proof that this is true in the abstract is to be found in the life-work of such men as Messrs. R. McAlister & Sons.

The business of timber, hardware, and general builders' merchant, and contractor which is conducted by Mr. John Hardy has been established in the City for about fifteen years.

During the past two or three years it has, with the City, made rapid strides, which have necessitated the erection, in Printing Office Street, of large and commodious premises, and the establishment in Church Street of a unique show-room.

The Printing Office Street premises, which are surmounted by the famous sky-sign, consist of warehouses, workshops, and offices of the business, while adjoining them, a convenient suite of offices, known as Hardy's Chambers, have been erected, which are at present occupied by people in various professions. The warehouses are stocked to overflowing with every conceivable kind of goods necessary to the building and house-decorating trade.

The new range of workshops now in course of construction are intended to cope with the ever-increasing demand, and by the time these pages see the light, will be replete with the latest inventions in labour-saving machinery.

As business premises, the whole block of buildings in Printing Office Street ranks with the finest in Maritzburg, and is an evidence of the success which has attended the business.

The progressive spirit evinced by Mr. Hardy has done much to improve the architectural style of Maritzburg, both in connection with the conduct of his business and in his career as a Municipal Councillor.

The chemists and druggists of the City take a deservedly high rank in their profession, and would compare favourably as a class with their co-workers anywhere in the world.

In dealing with them in this section of the work, we naturally turn first to the long-established business of Messrs. Turner & Co., which was established in the very beginning of Maritzburg's history. The present firm has fully maintained the traditions of the past, and has done much to raise the dignity of the profession to the high standard it occupies at present.

Messrs. Stantial & Allerston also occupy a prominent position ; and it is to the enterprise of the firm that the medical profession of Maritzburg is indebted for the introduction of that wonderful development of modern photography, the " Rontgen Rays."

It will be remembered by those who have read the previous chapters of this history that in the old days, when the Boers were struggling with the warriors of Dingaan, they made a vow and a covenant with the Lord to the effect that if He would vouchsafe them the victory over their savage adversaries, they would erect a House to the honour and glory of His name. That vow was fulfilled, and a building was erected at the corner of Church Street and the Market Square.

Not only was this the first place of worship in Natal, but it became the mother church of South-eastern Africa.

For many years it was the religious centre of the country. On the completion of the present church, which stands beside it, the original building became the manse, but later on was leased under special restrictions as a place of business.

In the rapid advance of the rest of the City it was overlooked and fell into disrepair, until Mr. Thomas Hannah took it over for the purpose of establishing himself in it as a chemist and druggist. With indomitable energy he speedily transformed the historic, but nevertheless dilapidated, structure into a first-class pharmaceutical establishment. Doctors' consulting rooms and work-rooms for the preparation of several valued proprietary medicines, such as Hannah's sarsaparilla, headache powders, antibilious pills, croup syrup, etc., are added.

Notwithstanding his apparent youth, Mr. Hannah has been connected with the dispensing and family chemist business for over twelve years. In every respect he is a worthy occupant of the celebrated structure he now holds.

Possessed of untiring energy and pluck, two qualities which are essential in a new country, he has succeeded in creating not only a successful business in the City, but in establishing himself as the principal chemist in the town of Ladysmith, and when his aerated water machinery is set up, will no doubt secure the bulk of the mineral water trade in Klip River County. Here, also, he has fitted up a first-class consulting room, where the three principal doctors of the county may be consulted.

INTERIOR OF MESSRS. TURNER AND CO.'S ESTABLISHMENT

Turner & Company, chemists and wholesale druggists. The above illustration represents the interior of the retail department of Messrs. Turner & Company's drug store, a spacious and lofty apartment, measuring 33ft. x 30ft., handsomely furnished and fitted.

The premises are situated in the centre of the City of Pietermaritzburg, immediately opposite the new Colonial Offices, and are replete with every modern convenience for the dispensing of physicians' prescriptions, whilst the stocks of invalids' requisites, surgical appliances, photographic goods, perfumery, &c., &c., are large and varied. The upper storey is devoted to the wholesale department, and here orders are constantly being made up and despatched to all parts of South Africa.

The firm was first established in the year 1873, by Mr. J. C. Bullock who was Quartermaster-Sergeant of the Natal Carbineers, and was killed in the fatal attack on the camp at Isandhlwana during the Zulu War, on the 22nd January, 1879.

Mr. W. O. Turner entered into partnership with Mr. Bullock in the year 1875, and has ever since the death of the latter continued to carry on and develop the business under the title of Turner & Company.

The firm has acquired an enviable reputation, and its business is ever increasing in both the wholesale and retail departments; in fact, it has grown with the town, and has kept thoroughly abreast with the times.

Mr. Robert Fuller, who conducts an important estabment in the centre of the City, is also widely and popularly known as one who spares no effort to carry out in a perfect and satisfactory manner that portion of the sacred art of healing which falls within the sphere of a chemist and druggist.

No work in the City of Maritzburg, or, in fact, in the Colony of Natal, would be complete without a reference to the person and the firm of Mr. Paul Henwood, who must be regarded as one of those who have fought in the forefront of the battle of progress which has raged since the beginning of the Colony to the present day. It would be hard to say where the firm has not either directly or indirectly established a business or influenced trade. It would take pages to enumerate the scope of the firm, or deal with the extent of its operations. But it is the City branch with which we have to deal in this work. Established in 1862, it has steadily increased in influence, until to-day it may be described as one of the most important institutions of its kind in the City. The large and varied stock of ironmongery, agricultural implements, and general goods of that description defies any attempt at a detailed description, while the stock of silver and electro-plate ware is equal to any held in South Africa.

Farmers, householders, retail dealers, and so on will find they will supply their wants, be they ever so large or small, at prices which will compare with any prevailing in the Colony.

One of the attractions of Church Street is undoubtedly the fine show room of Messrs. Clifford & Smith, importers, furniture dealers, and upholsterers. The intending purchaser will find, however extensive his wants may be, that the firm can cope with them on a satisfactory basis as regards style, quality, and price.

As a Home buyer of furniture, household accessories, and such-like commodities, Mr. Clifford has had a large experience; while Mr. Smith's practical knowledge of cabinet and mattress making is almost unrivalled in the City.

In addition to the care and skill which are lavished on the departments before mentioned, the firm makes a speciality of picture-frame making, and is prepared at the shortest possible notice to produce artistic and well-finished frames in every style of art.

Owing to the extensive nature of the firm's operations throughout the Colony, it is in a position to furnish on satisfactory terms any habitation from a castle to a cottage, and, better still, to pack, deliver, and set up the purchased articles with the utmost promptitude.

The shifting population, which is incidental to a garrison town, should not lose sight of the fact that the firm has created a department for the supply on hire or purchase of furniture suitable to their requirements.

Those furnishing homes, either temporary or permanent, should make a point of consulting the firm before incurring heavy expenditure elsewhere.

If the prosperity of a town or a city may be gauged by the enterprise and industry of its merchants, we would not hesitate to cite Messrs. Mason & Broadbent as a fair type of the description of firm which does as much to maintain the position of an important British Colony as the politician and the soldier.

Without the enterprise of our merchants, the two latter mentioned would have but scant opportunity for the exercise and display of their abilities.

Messrs. Mason & Broadbent are no recent arrivals on the scene of activity, the events of which are woven through the pages of this history.

Nearly fifty years ago, before Maritzburg had a recognised existence, the senior member of the firm first appeared upon the scene. It was not until 1891, however, that the firm took its present form and occupied the leading position which it now holds.

Situated at 287, Church Street, the front stores, which are piled with merchandise, convey even then but an inadequate idea of the vast stock which is stored away in four or five adjacent warehouses. Notwithstanding this accommodation, the extensive operations of the firm have necessitated the construction of new and handsome frontal premises.

To attempt an enumeration of the scope and extent of the stock in all its varieties which may here be found would require another volume. Suffice it to say, that every requisite in the building, ironmongery, and brushware trade is available. No Alladin's lamp is required to satisfy every wish of the intending purchaser if that ubiquitous and ever-obliging member of the firm (Mr. Broadbent) is at hand, and he is rarely absent.

Whether it is a wholesale order for the stocking of an up-country emporium, or a modest order for a hank of sail twine, presto—it is done.

Keenly alive to the requirements of the Colonial trade, the firm has made a special study of the art of buying, and the result is that nowhere in South Africa can the customer find a better depôt than in the establishment of Messrs. Mason & Broadbent.

In previous chapters of this work much has been said on the founding and building of this City, but as yet we have not touched on the clothing of its inhabitants.

On this subject there are few better authorities to be found than Messrs. Taylor & Fowler, clothiers, hatters, hosiers, and general outfitters, Church Street, two doors above Chapel Street, with branch establishments at Ladysmith and Dundee. This old-established business has steadily kept pace with the progress of the City.

It has been said by some writer that no conscientious effort to do well can ever fail to meet its due reward, which is a wide-spread appreciation and cordial support, both of which are fully enjoyed by the firm. Messrs. Taylor &

Fowler in their extensive premises have a grand display and stock of clothing made up in high-class style, almost equal to their tailor-made.

The firm has an immense stock of fancy tweeds, navy and black serge and worsted suitings, and fancy trouserings and dress suitings. Patterns are sent to any part of the country. Having a staff of practical tailors and reliable cutters on the premises, they can guarantee workmanship, style, and fit. Those desiring it, may, through them, avail themselves of London tailor-made suits. They have a big range of patterns in all the latest cloths, and measures are taken here and sent direct to their London tailors, and delivered with dispatch. They have a large and well-assorted stock of gentlemen's walking, cycling, riding, shooting, football, and working boots, in all shades of tan and black, and all qualities; also boys' and youths' in light and heavy makes for walking and school wear. Also, ladies' boots and shoes in great variety, quality, and price, in tan and black, and a good stock of girls' boots and shoes in all styles. In children's strapped tan, patent, and black shoes they cannot be beaten. Exceptional value in juvenile clothing and outfitting. They have weekly shipments of the latest ties and collars and hats for travellers; all requisites for comfort at reasonable prices; shawl rugs, seal rugs, ulsters, mackintoshes, ladies' and gentlemen's portmanteaux, Gladstone brief bags, holdalls, etc., in large varieties. For cyclists: cycling suits, caps, and shoes; waterproof capes; ladies', gentlemen's, girls', and youths' bicycles, and all kinds of latest accessories kept in stock. For pedestrians: suits, stockings, boots, caps, &c. For the rainy season they keep a grand stock of waterproofs, sewn throughout and every one guaranteed; umbrellas in ladies' and gentlemen's, walking sticks and overalls in great varieties.

By careful buying and judicial management, they are enabled, both as regards price and quality, to defy competition.

Long established as the firm is, it appears but seemly that they should occupy an honoured place within the covers of a work which is devoted to the treatment or such institutions as go to maintain and support the City.

Mr. J. C. Baumann, baker and confectioner, conducts his business in Boshoff Street.

Commencing in a very modest style, he has steadily and gradually developed with the City, until at the present moment he conducts a large and prosperous business, having the liberal support of the general public.

He has carried the art of his trade to a high state of perfection, and has established a wide popularity in the fancy department of his business, such as bridescakes and general confectionery.

One of the reasons of Mr. Baumann's success is that he uses especial yeast of his own preparation, and the other is his close attention to the details of his business, coupled with a kindliness of disposition, which render him as popular as he is successful.

The Imperial Hotel : On the 24th of May, 1898, this popular hotel celebrated the twentieth anniversary of its establishment in the City. In common with several other institutions which we have dealt with in this volume, it has shared, for weal and woe, the vicissitudes of the City life. In the beginning of its career, the whole establishment consisted of about twelve rooms, lighted in primitive fashion by paraffin lamps. Now it would be difficult indeed to recognise in the present beautifully-appointed hostelry the slightest trace of the old order, saving and excepting the kindly hostess, Mrs. Thresh, who has contrived to remain, as she ever has been, the most popular and widely-known hotel proprietress in the City.

At the time of writing, March, 1898, the hotel consists of sixty-five apartments, with three sitting-rooms, three dining-rooms, and smoking room. In additions to these there are twelve bathrooms, two kitchens, two storerooms, two baggage rooms, and the usual offices.

Large and commodious stables and carriage-houses occupy the back premises, while the lavatories and sanitary arrangements are perfect.

At the present time, new wings and blocks of buildings are in course of construction, which, when completed, will make the hotel one of the most perfect in South Africa. The new wing, which is almost finished, is devoted principally to bedrooms and bathrooms, and the traveller must be indeed unreasonable who could find any fault with the spacious, well-ventilated and luxurious apartments. Every necessity seems to have been catered for, and whether the guest is travelling alone, with his family, or his valet, he will find every convenience provided. The hotel has been fitted with electric light throughout, and waits the completion of the installation promised by the Corporation.

In order to meet the convenience of guests, a commodious drag meets every registered passenger train, and, when desired, vehicles are procurable wherein to visit the various points of interest in the vicinity of the City.

The reputation which the hotel has deservedly earned during its twenty years of existence, may well be envied far and wide, and its praises have been recorded in more than one important book of travel from the pens of political, journalistic, and social magnates.

A list of the notabilities who have been guests of the hotel would form interesting reading did space permit of its insertion here. The following names, however, will serve to indicate a few of them :—

LIST OF VISITORS.

Mark Twain.	Sir Garnet Wolseley.
Max O'Rell.	Lord Cantelope.
H. M. Stanley, Esq., M.P.	General Tucker, C.B.
Signor Foli.	General Cox, C.B.
Madame Albani.	Mr. Justice Williams.
Madame Trebelli.	Capt. Walter.
Lady and Sir Charles Hallé.	Mr. Sims Reeves.
The Marquis of Devonshire.	Bishop Colenso, D.D.
Dr. Kingsley.	Sir B. Stone, M.P.
Mr. Balfour.	Col. Dalgety.
Sir Evelyn Wood.	

Amongst the curiosities of interest which Mrs. Thresh has contrived to collect are a magnificent display of African antelope and big game horns, while in the passage, and now constituting a seat, are the veritable stocks which were used by the Boers to confine and exhibit the British prisoners who fell into their hands at the taking of the Point during the Anglo-Boer War in Natal, 1842.

In conclusion, it is perfectly safe to say that the tourist, let him come from where he may, will find in the Imperial Hotel a home-like resting place, which will compare favourably with anything of the kind in the world.

Amongst the millers and corn dealers of the City, the firm of Messrs. W. H. Walker & Co. has, though but recently commenced business, acquired a well-deserved reputation for fair dealing with those who entrust their affairs to them. Their two places of business, one in Commercial Road, near St. Saviour's Cathedral, and the other in Longmarket Street, near the Plough Hotel, are centres of activity and bustle.

Here one may see on the one hand loads of grain arriving from the country, and on the other milled product leaving for the various depôts for sale.

Mr. Walker, the senior partner of the firm, was for many years associated with the firm of Messrs. R. Mason & Son, and both during that period and subsequently has acquired a thorough knowledge of a business which is as vital to the welfare of the Colony as the prosperity of the farmer, who depends on him for his returns.

Notwithstanding the dull times, the firm is adding still further to its already extensive premises and plant, and it may confidently be stated that a long and prosperous career is opening out before the firm.

Mr. D. Nicolson, who is well known for his enterprise and attention to business, commenced in the City, at No. 8, Temple Street, about June, 1897. Finding the rapid increase of his engagements necessitated more accommodation, he has lately acquired the extensive premises, formerly occupied by Messrs. W. Muir & Sons, 319, Church Street, where, assisted by a large staff of competent workmen, he carries on the trade of a builder, contractor, and timber merchant.

On inspection of the works we found that in addition to the wood-working plant already on the premises, there is now erected a very complete machine for striking mouldings of different descriptions, tonguing, grooving, &c.

Mr. Nicolson's South African experience is long and varied. In addition to large contracts with the Military authorities at Fort Napier, he has been associated with the building of the Memorial Church, Y.M.C.A. Hall, Catholic Sanatorium, &c., &c. And is at present engaged on the additions to St. Saviour's Cathedral, new frontage to Messrs. W. H. Griffin & Co.'s premises, and the erection of several large dwelling houses for private customers.

We noticed a large and varied stock of timber and building materials of all descriptions.

Amongst the watchmakers, jewellers, and opticians of the City, Messrs. Sckwake, Watt & Co. take a deservedly high place. Their establishment at 286, Longmarket Street, facing the Market Square, is not only beautifully furnished, but contains one of the finest-selected stocks to be found in the Colony. The business is an old-established one, it having been commenced in 1880 by Mr. Bernard Schwake in premises adjoining the Plough Hotel. For 18 years business was conducted in this place, but within the past few months it was found imperatively necessary, by reason of the increased patronage of the public, to remove to the present handsome premises which it occupies. Six years ago Mr. Schwake, the senior partner, removed to London to act as buyer for the firm, and is, by his South African experience, enabled to obtain direct from the manufacturers goods which not only suit the trade, but, through personal selection, are of the best quality, and can be offered at prices lower than could otherwise be done. In the optical department, the firm lays itself out to supply any description of spectacles, pince-nez, etc., to suit all sights, and carry out doctors' and oculists' prescriptions with the greatest care. The horological and jewellery departments, as well as the general business of the firm, are conducted by Mr. Henry Niesewand, the sole South African partner, who has achieved a wide popularity by reason of his unremitting attention to the requirements of his customers.

List of Mayors of Pietermaritzburg.

SINCE THE INCORPORATION OF THE BOROUGH IN 1854.

1854—D. D. Buchanan.
1855—D. B. Scott.
1856—P. Ferreira.
1857—W. Leathern and G. Thompson.
1858—J. Archbell.
1859—J. W. Akerman.
1860—J. Archbell.
1861—J. Archbell.
1862—J. Archbell.
1863—J. Archbell.
1864—E. Tomlinson.
1865—E. Tomlinson.
1866—E. Tomlinson.
1867—S. Williams.
1868—S. Williams.
1869—S. Williams and J. Russom.
1870—E. Tomlinson and W. George.
1871—W. George.
1872—P. Davis, sen.
1873—P. Davis, sen.
1874—Henry Pepworth.
1875—John Fleming.

1876—John Fleming
1877—W Francis.
1878—W. Francis.
1879—P. Davis, sen.
1880—A. W. Kershaw.
1881—John Roseveare.
1882—S. Williams.
1883—H. Griffin.
1884—E. Owen.
1885—E. Owen.
1886—J. J. Chapman.
1887—J. J. Chapman.
1887—J. J. Chapman.
1889—E. S. T. Stantial.
1890—W. E. Bale.
1891—Richard Mason.
1892—Richard Mason.
1893—W E. Bale.
1894—P Carbis.
1895—C. G. Levy.
1896—P. F. Payn.
1897—T. W. Woodhouse
1898—G. J. Macfarlane.

TOWN CLERKS.

1854 to 1861—James Raw.
1861 to 1879—E. Buchanan.

1879 to 1883—E. Wiltshire.
1883 to Date—S. Stranack.

Cab Stands and Cab Fares.

STANDS.

Notice is hereby given, that the Town Council has appointed the undermentioned places as Cab Stands, during pleasure, under the provisions of By-Law No. 335. Not more than six cabs will be allowed at any stand :—

1. Commercial Road, in front of Crown Hotel.
2. Commercial Road, between Fountain and Police Station.
3. Church Street, in front of Standard Bank.
4. Church Street, in front of St. Peter's Cathedral.
5. Chapel Street, in front of Theatre Royal.
6. Church Street, above Gate of Court Gardens.

N.B.—Cabs are not confined to the authorised stands between 9 p.m. and 6 a.m.

TARIFF OF FARES.

Fares by Distance.—For any Licensed Vehicle, when employed between the Bridges and the Camp Gardens. For a single Adult Passenger, per mile or fraction thereof, 1s.; for each additional Passenger, per mile or fraction thereof, 6d.

Fares by Time.—For one and not more than two Adults, 4s. per hour; for every additional Adult, 1s. per hour.

N.B.—In every case, each Person over the age of 12 years shall be reckoned as an Adult. Half-fares only shall be charged for Persons under the age of 12 years.

Double Fares.—Double Fares may be charged between 10 p.m. and 6 a.m.

Charge for Luggage.—For each Adult Passenger 30lbs. of luggage is allowed free of charge.

Number of Passengers.—The number of passengers allowed to each four-wheeled cab is four inside and one outside; to each two-wheeled cab, two inside.

The following By-laws are published for general information :—

By-law 329.—" When hired by time, the driver in charge of the vehicle shall be bound to drive at a proper rate of speed, say not less than *five* miles an hour, unless requested to drive at a slower rate."

By-law 330.—" Every vehicle registered for public hire, standing in the public street, shall be deemed to be plying for hire, and the person in charge of such vehicle shall not refuse to accept engagement unless actually engaged or hired at the time. Written or other evidence of being hired must be produced at the time by the person in charge of the vehicle if required."

By-law 337.—" Any driver of an omnibus, cab, or hackney-carriage, or any jinriksha-puller, who shall demand from any passenger more than the fare legally chargeable under these By-laws, shall be liable to a penalty not exceeding Two Pounds Sterling, and in default of payment to imprisonment for a period not exceeding one month, with or without hard labour."

By-law 338.—" Any person who shall wilfully avoid or attempt to avoid payment of the fare legally chargeable under these By-laws shall be liable to a penalty not exceeding Two Pounds Sterling, and in default of payment to imprisonment for a period not exceeding one month, with or without hard labour."

By-law 340.—" The animals employed in the working of all hired vehicles shall be at all times kept in good condition."

By Order of the Mayor and Council,

STEPHEN STRANACK,
Town Clerk.

Town Office, Pietermaritzburg,
August, 1895.

Jinriksha Fares and Stands.

FARES.

Jinriksha Fares shall not exceed the following Tariff :—For every person 3d. per half-mile or portion thereof.

Fares by Time shall be.—1s. 6d. per hour for one person, or 2s. 3d. per hour for two persons. One or two Children under 12 years of age to count as One Person.

Between the hours of 11 p.m. and 6 a.m. Fares shall not be chargeable at more than Double Rate.

The following By-Laws are published for information :—

By-law 330.—"Every vehicle registered for public hire, stand-in the public street, shall be deemed to be plying for hire, and the person in charge of such vehicle shall not refuse to accept engagement unless actually engaged or hired at the time. Written or other evidence of being hired must be produced at the time by the person in charge of the vehicle if required."

By-law 337.—"Any driver of an omnibus, cab, or hackney-carriage, or any jinriksha-puller, who shall demand from any passenger more than the fare legally chargeable under these By-laws, shall be liable to a penalty not exceeding Two Pounds sterling, and in default of payment to imprisonment for a period not exceeding one month, with or without hard labour."

By-law 338.—"Any person who shall wilfully avoid or attempt to avoid payment of the fare legally chargeable under these By-Laws shall be liable to a penalty not exceeding Two Pounds sterling, and in default of payment to imprisonment for a period not exceeding one month, with or without hard labour."

STANDS.

The Council have defined Riksha Stands for the convenience of the public, and these are now placed on record for general information, as follows :—

	No. of Rikshas		No. of Rikshas
Church Street—		*Longmarket Street—*	
Railway Station (outside jurisdiction)		Burchell's	5
		Cathedral Grounds	10
Soldiers' Institute	5	Police Station	10
Medical Hall	5	Girls' School	5
St. Peter's Cathedral	7		
Frank Stevens'	3	*Chapel Street—*	
Telegraph Office	7	Griffin's	10
Colonial Offices (suspended temporarily)	7	Theatre	10
Town Hall	10	*Commercial Road—*	
Market Square (opposite Francis & Sons)	10	Market Gardens	10
		Whitelaw's	5
Longmarket Street—		*Boshoff Street—*	
Government House	5	Wesleyan Church	10
Natal Brewery	10		

And at places of Public Entertainment within the above-mentioned limits when Entertainments are going on, at the discretion of the authorities.

The boundaries of Riksha Stands will be marked on the kerbstone in each case in due course.

IRELAND & CO.,

Clothiers, Outfitters, Hatters, and Tailors,

ESTABLISHED 1862,

AND STILL MAINTAINING

PREMIER POSITION.

First Quality Goods in all Departments

FOR **GENT,'S, YOUTHS', AND BOYS' WEAR.**

227, CHURCH STREET

PIETERMARITZBURG.

GRAND SHOW OF
NEW GOODS
FOR ALL SEASONS AT
WM. ROGERSON'S

French Millinery
Latest Paris Shapes in Untrimmed Hats.
Choicest of Dress Materials.
Dressmaking in all its Branches.
Lovely Silks.
Newest Trimmings.

NOVELTIES in Ladies' Capes, Mantles, Tea Gowns, Blouses, Costumes, Skirts, Children's Hats, Dresses, Ladies' Umbrellas, Sunshades, Laces, Ribbons, Hosiery, and a

MAGNIFICENT STOCK OF
HIGH-CLASS DRAPERY.

All of the Best, and Lowest Prices,
AT
WM. ROGERSON'S,
Church Street, Maritzburg.

MICHAELHOUSE,

Boarding and Day School for Boys,

PIETERMARITZBURG.

RECTOR : THE REV. CANON TODD, M.A., B.Sc.

MASTERS :—Mr. TRON, London University.
Mr. DOBREE, B.A., Jesus College, Cambridge.
Mr. Hannah, St. Mary's Hall, Oxford.

ST. ANNE'S DIOCESAN COLLEGE,
MARITZBURG.

Visitor : RIGHT REV. THE LORD BISHOP OF NATAL.

Lady Warden   : : :   Miss BROWNE.
Head Mistress : : :   Miss HEATON.

Assisted by an Efficient Staff of Resident Mistresses.

Pupils are prepared for the Oxford Local, the Cape University Elementary and Matriculation, the S. Andrew's L.L.A., and the Cape University and Trinity College Music Examinations.

A Branch School in connection with the above will be opened in Dundee, Natal, in August, 1898.

MISS MOORE, HEAD MISTRESS.

VISITORS—DON'T FAIL TO CALL ON

TAYLOR & FOWLER,

THE CITY

CLOTHIERS AND OUTFITTERS,

TAILORS, HATTERS, AND HOSIERS,

AND BOOT AND SHOE FACTORS.

A Speciality—*Juvenile Clothing.*

Weekly Shipments of the Latest Ties, Collars, &c., &c., Up-to-Date.

Ladies', Gent.'s, Girls', and Youths' BICYCLES and Accessories kept in Stock.

TAYLOR & FOWLER,

PIETERMARITZBURG, LADYSMITH,

AND DUNDEE, NATAL.

v.

MALLET & CO.,

Corner of Longmarket Street and Commercial Road,

Direct Importers of

GENERAL DRAPERY, AND BOYS' AND YOUTHS' CLOTHING.

Best Quality, combined with Lowest Prices.

H. J. HARRISON

(Late HUNT BROTHERS.)

WEST END SUPPLY STORES,

64, CHURCH STREET, MARITZBURG.

FISH, FRUIT, & VEGETABLE DEPOT.

TO COUNTRY STOREKEEPERS.

Before going elsewhere call for Quotations from

E. G. MENDENHALL, GENERAL IMPORTER,

142, CHURCH STREET,

PIETERMARITZBURG.

ALEX. OGILVIE,

DIRECT IMPORTER OF BOOTS AND SHOES.

Waverley Boot Stores,

243, LONGMARKET STREET, PIETERMARITZBURG.

Telegrams "MOWAT."   Telephone: No. 111.

MOWAT & STILL,

97 & 103, CHURCH STREET,

PIETERMARITZBURG, NATAL,

**GENERAL CONTRACTORS,
DIRECT IMPORTERS,
TIMBER MERCHANTS,
AND BUILDERS.**

RAILWAY CONSTRUCTION CONTRACTORS.
CONTRACTORS TO NATAL GOVERNMENT RAILWAY DEPARTMENT.
CONTRACTORS TO NATAL HARBOUR DEPARTMENT.
CONTRACTORS TO NATAL AGRICULTURAL DEPARTMENT.
CONTRACTORS TO NATAL CITY CORPORATION, ETC.

Estimates for all classes of Buildings.

Land Bought and Buildings Erected to suit Clients.

For Sale — All description of Building Material, Galvanised Iron, Builders' Ironmongery, Deals, Scantlings, Doors, Windows, Mouldings, Skirtings, Flooring, Ceilings, Pine Boards, Pitch and Oregon Pine, Teak, etc., etc.

Free Stone Sills, Verandah Bases, and every description of Stonework supplied; White's and other brands of Cement at lowest Market Rates.

CLIFFORD & SMITH,

Furniture Dealers,

CABINETMAKERS AND UPHOLSTERERS.

FURNITURE REPAIRED AND PICTURES FRAMED.

New Furniture arriving by every Mail.

ALWAYS ON HAND

A Few lines in Second-hand Furniture; also Crockery, Glassware, Carpets, etc.

CLIFFORD & SMITH,
252, CHURCH STREET,
PIETERMARITZBURG.

J. RAW & CO.

295, CHURCH STREET, PIETERMARITZBURG, AND COMMERCIAL ROAD, DURBAN.

THE CITY AND COUNTRY AUCTIONEERS, APPRAISERS, LAND AND ESTATE AGENTS,

GENERAL MERCHANTS AND IMPORTERS.

Auctioneers to the Imperial Government, the Howick, Nottingham Road, Mooi River, and Richmond Farmers' Associations.

Sales held every Saturday of Horses, Cattle, Sheep, Wagons, Carriages, etc., etc., at their Stands, Market Square, commencing at 10 o'clock a.m.

Land Sales held regularly.

Furniture Sales held in the City and Country.

Country Sales of Cattle, Horses, &c., arranged for on the shortest notice.

Cattle sent for Sale can be herded and kraaled free of charge.

Cash Settlements immediately after Sales.

J. RAW & CO., Wholesale Wine and Spirit Merchants. Large Stocks of Brandies, Whiskies, English and Colonial Ales and Stout, always on hand.

Kop's Non-Alcholic Ale and Stout.

Groceries and Oilman's Stores of all descriptions kept in Stock.

Tartarian and other Seed Oats always in Stock.

Cocksfoot Grass Seed.

Agents for Fison's Chemical Fertilizers for Potatoes, Forage, Mealies, Fruit, and all Vegetable and Root Crops.

Fison's Extra Quality Dissolved Bones.

Saint Raphael Wine for Invalids.

J. RAW & CO. are the Sole Agents in Natal for the **Champion Mower and Reaper.** The Best Machine yet made. Call and Inspect them before purchasing elsewhere. Prices Moderate.

Testimonial from Mr. J. Arnold, of Springfield, New England, near Maritzburg:—

"I purchased of you a 'Champion Mower,' which I have had in use ever since. It does most excellent work. I have put it into several different classes of Grass, and it works most satisfactorily.

"I have used a quantity of different Mowers, but never yet had one to equal the 'Champion.'

"Anyone wishing to see the Machine at work may come any day to my farm."

CITY PUBLIC SUPPLY STORES.
126—130, CHURCH STREET, MARITZBURG.
ALFRED GRIX,
Established 1874.

Direct Importer of

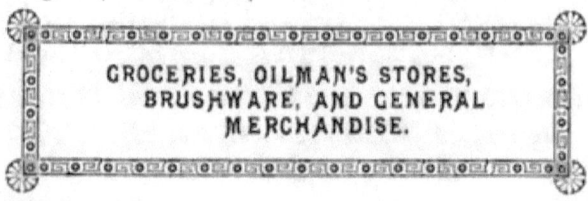

GROCERIES, OILMAN'S STORES, BRUSHWARE, AND GENERAL MERCHANDISE.

ALFRED GRIX is noted for keeping High-Class Goods, selling at Lowest Prices, Importing only Fresh Goods and having the Largest and most Varied Selection to be found in the City.

ADDRESS:
ALFRED GRIX, City Public Supply Stores, Pietermaritzburg.

MODES DE PARIS.

ARTISTIC MILLINERY.

Ladies visiting 210, Church Street, Pietermaritzburg, will find a host of exclusive designs, and always the most recherche Millinery. Personally conducted by

MME. HAMER-CALVERT.

HOWICK FALLS HOTEL

(NEAREST HOTEL TO THE FALLS.)

Pleasantly situated in the Village of Howick, within one minute's walk of the Falls, Court House, Post and Telegraph Office.

There are 40 Bedrooms (27 of which are on the Upper Floor), Balcony all round. Private Suites of Rooms; Smoking, Music, and Ladies' Rooms; Billiard Room and Bar separate from Hotel; Dark Room and Bath Rooms, with water laid on; Perfect Sanitary Arrangements; and all the other Accessories of a well-appointed Establishment. Traps and Saddle Horses on Hire. Picnic Parties driven to the Karkloof Falls, &c. An excellent Cuisine. The Best Brands of Wines, Spirits, and Cigars kept. A Covered Conveyance meets all Day Trains, and by arrangement the Night Mails.

M. SIMONS.

Telegraphic Address; "*FALLS, HOWICK.*"

The Howick Falls (one minute from the Hotel), with a sheer drop of 308 feet, are said to be the second highest unbroken Falls in the World.

VISITORS THAT HAVE BEEN AT THE HOTEL.

Lady Florence Dixie, 1881.	Cecil Rhodes.	Marquis of Devonshire
Sir Beaumont Dixie.	Lionel Phillips.	Dr. Kingsley.
Sir Charles Halle.	Herman Eckstein.	Mr. Balfour.
Lady Halle.	Frederick Eckstein.	H. W. L. or W. L. H Lawson, connected with the *Daily News*.
Signor Foli.	Bishop Colenso.	
Madame Trebelli.	Miss Margeurite Macintyre.	
Charles Santley.	Mark Twain.	Sims Reeves.
H. M. Stanley.	Lord Cantelupe.	His Hon. Paul Kruger, Transvaal President.

P. HENWOOD, SON,

SOUTTER & CO.,

Furnishing & General Ironmongers,

AGRICULTURAL IMPLEMENTS

AND

FARM REQUISITES.

CHURCH STREET

PIETERMARITZBURG, NATAL,

DURBAN, PRETORIA, BARBERTON,
JOHANNESBURG, KROMDRAAI, AND KIMBERLEY.

WILLIAMS & LAMBERT,
WHITE HOUSE,
MARITZBURG,

ARE NOTED FOR

High-Class Men.'s Youths' and Boys' Outfitting.

SPECIALITIES :

The A1 Clothing to Measure.—Surpassing all other makes. Fit, Style, and Workmanship.

Boys' Clothing.—A large stock always on hand and the latest Styles received by every Mail.

Boys' Blouses.—A Choice Selection always in Stock, and our Buyers ship us the NEWEST PRODUCTIONS as they appear in the Markets.

Boys' Hats and Caps.—The best Assortment in the Colony, and always up-to-date.

Boys' Shirts, Boys' Hosiery, Boys' Knickers.

Cellular Clothing.—Far and away the Best Clothing for the South African Climate. The sale is an ever-increasing one, and we hold one of the Largest Stocks in South Africa.

Gent.'s Ties.—Our Stocks of Ties will always be found replete with the very Latest Novelties.

Gent.'s Hats and Caps.—In this Department we lead ; others follow ; and our Prices are lower than the lowest.

Gent.'s Hosiery.—The Best Makes only Stocked.

All our Goods Marked in PLAIN FIGURES, and PERSONAL ATTENTION at all times.

WILLIAMS & LAMBERT, WHITE HOUSE,
Opposite the Cathedral, Maritzburg.

HILTON COLLEGE.

The object of this School is to provide for Colonial Boys the kind of training which is given at Home by the "Public Schools."

The Masters are University and Public School men.

The Site is particularly Healthy, being on an estate of nearly 2,000 acres, 1,500 feet above Maritzburg, and among the finest Scenery of the Midlands of Natal.

The School has an excellent record of 26 years in Work and Games, and keeps touch with its old members by means of a strong Hiltonian Society.

HENRY VAUGHAN ELLIS,
HEADMASTER.

PIETERMARITZBURG HIGH SCHOOL FOR GIRLS.

Principal: Miss A. E. ROWE, Late Newnham College, Cambridge, and for eight years Lady Principal of the Girls' Collegiate School, Maritzburg; First-class Honours Certificate, Woman's Cambridge, &c.

A large staff of Resident and Visiting Teachers of the highest qualifications.

Miss Rowe has had long experience of management in English, French, and German Public and Private Schools.

Pupils are prepared for the Junior and Senior Oxford Local, Natal Teachers' Certificate, and various Music and Art Examinations.

It is intended during the year 1898 to move the School into commodious buildings, specially erected for the purpose, on a 30 to 40 acre plot of land, some three miles from the City, adjoining the Zwaartkop Road Station.

Trains are both frequent and convenient, enabling Visiting Teachers and Day Scholars to attend regularly.

The site is pleasant and healthy, situated several hundred feet above the town, commanding a magnificient view of the City, and excellent provision is made for a large number of Boarders.

J. MERRYWEATHER & SONS,

Wagonmakers,

Blacksmiths, &c.

Supply Wagons of Every Description on Shortest Notice and at Low Prices; Workmanship and Material Guaranteed. Tip Carts, Light Delivery Carts; also Light Spring Carts, suitable for Drapers and Grocers.

TROLLEYS (*both Heavy and Light*), **WHEELBARROWS.**

All Sizes of Wheels In Stock or Made to Order.

Sneezewood, Stinkwood, Stinkwood Shafts Sawn or Bent to Shape, Forgings, either for Ploughs, Wagons, or Mowing Machines.

Machinery Repaired.

SCREW CUTTING.   WOOD AND IRON TURNING.

PLANING AND SAWING OF EVERY DESCRIPTION.

LOGS SAWN TO ORDER.

352, CHURCH STREET,

PIETERMARITZBURG.

ST. CHARLES' GRAMMAR SCHOOL.

Situated in a very healthy place, between Loop Street and Longmarket Street, gives accommodation to a certain number of Boarders, and to Day Pupils.

It is placed under the patronage and direction of the Right Reverend Dr. Jolivet.

Boys are prepared for the Cape University, Natal Civil Service, and other Examinations. Besides, every attention is paid to the moral tone and general conduct of the boys, with a view to their becoming honourable and gentlemanly.

For particulars apply to—

The Revd. FATHER DELALLE, D.D., Principal.

J.M.J.
CONVENT OF THE HOLY FAMILY.

PIETERMARITZBURG.
YOUNG LADIES' BOARDING AND DAY SCHOOLS.
KINDERGARTEN—OR SELECT INFANT SCHOOL FOR BOTH SEXES.

Established 1878.

The course of Instruction comprises a Solid English Education; the French Language; English and French Literature; Vocal and Instrumental Music; and every species of Plain and Fancy Needlework

Pupils are prepared for the various Local Examinations in English and Music, according to the wishes of their Parents.

The School possesses extensive grounds, and is situated in one of the healthiest parts of the City.

For terms and particulars apply to—

THE MOTHER SUPERIOR.

WILLIAM MELDRUM

(ESTABLISHED 1859).

Aerated Water Manufacturer,

23—29, HENRIETTA STREET,

PIETERMARITZBURG.

Every description of High-class Aerated Waters Manufactured.

Best Quality Ingredients only used.

N.B.—Special Attention to Country Orders.

THE NATAL TANNING COMPANY, LTD.,
PIETERMARITZBURG

Telegraphic Address:
"*TANNING.*"

Works: On Banks of Umsindusi. Offices: 27, TIMBER STREET.

All kinds of Leather Manufactured from Natal Hides.

Sole Leather; Harness Leather; Machine Belting of all widths; Veldschoens in all Sizes, always on hand.

D. McDONALD,
GEAR FOUNDRY.
213, Pietermaritz Street.

Brickmaking Plant made to order, with all the Latest Improvements.

Castings made in Brass or Iron to patterns supplied.

Engineering and Blacksmithing in all its branches.

Forage or Hay Presses, Mealie Shellers, Single, Double, and Three-Furrow Ploughs, Harrows.

Land Rollers on hand or made at the Shortest Notice.

Ornamental Cast or Wrought Iron Work a Speciality.

SIMMER, JENKINS & CO.,
Drapers, Outfitters and General House Furnishers,
168 TO 174, LONGMARKET STREET, MARITZBURG.

GOOD!!

It's DERRETT'S
Mineral Waters,
Lemon Squash,
and

Cordials.

Pietermaritzburg, P.O. BOX 66.   Telegrams, "DERRETT."

CASTLE HOTEL, HOWICK.

Having been thoroughly renovated, is replete with every Home Comfort. Busses meet all Day Trains. Night Mail by Special Arrangement.

Telegraphic Address: "CASTLE," Howick.

For terms, apply to—

JAMES COLE, Proprietor

DAVID WHITELAW & SON,

PIETERMARITZBURG

and

JOHANNESBURG,

Wagon Builders, Blacksmiths, Wood-turners, and Timber Merchants,

Are the largest Manufactures in South Africa, and have always on hand a very large Stock of the following. Every Vehicle Guaranteed made of thoroughly seasoned Timber and best workmanship. Our Manufactures are of great repute throughout the whole of South Africa.

WAGONS—All sizes, for Oxen, Horses, Mules, and Donkeys.
SPRING TROLLEYS—In Twenty different Sizes and Kinds for one or more Horses.
BLOCK TROLLEYS—All Sizes.
SPRING DELIVERY VANS, SPRING CARTS, AND BUTCHERS' CARTS.
SCOTCH CARTS—For Horses, Mules, or Oxen.
HAND CARTS—Various Sizes.

Wagon, Cart, and Trolley Builders' Materials, comprising Timber of every description; Axles and Springs, Naves, Spokes, Felloes, and Felloe Rims, Bonds; Cape Cart, Spring Cart, and Scotch Cart Poles; Scotch Cart and Spring Cart Shafts, all sizes; Swinglebars for Dog-Carts, Mules, &c.; Neckbars, Table Legs, Sofa Feet, Finials, &c.; every description of Cabinet Turnings; American Hickory and Ash Planks, 2in., 3in. and 4in. thick; American Pine Shelving and Poplar Boards.

Photos and Price Lists on application to either of the undermentioned addresses.

Maritzburg Address : Box 105.   Johannesburg Address : Box 1629.
Telegrams : "WHITELAW."   Telegrams : "WHITELAW."

SOUTH AFRICAN BREWERIES, LIMITED.

NATAL BREWERY'S
(PIETERMARITZBURG)
Celebrated Sparkling Ales and Invalid Stout.

These Beers are Brewed from the very Best Materials only.

Supplied in Patent Screw Stoppered Quarts and Pints, or in Ordinary Corked Bottles.

LIGHT AND WHOLESOME. SPECIALLY SUITED FOR THE CLIMATE.

Delivered to all Parts of Natal; also to Cape Colony, Orange Free State, Transvaal, Zululand, and Delagoa Bay.

Supplied in Casks of all Sizes

Write for Quotations and Prices.

TRADE MARK.

Telegrams—"Brewery, Maritzburg." Pietermaritzburg, Longmarket Street, Telephone No. 70. Durban Agency, 432, West Street, Telephone No. 131. Ladysmith Depot, Ladysmith. Agencies at Eshowe and Harrismith.

HARVEY, GREENACRE & Co.,

225, CHURCH STREET,

MARITZBURG,

Importers of High-Class

Boots and Shoes.

F. G. BURCHELL,
(ESTABLISHED 1873.)

Commission, Livery, and Bait Stables.

Carriages, Cabs, and Saddle Horses on Hire, also Wedding Carriages and Dog-Carts.

HORSE DEALER IN ALL ITS BRANCHES.

ADDRESS:
TEMPLE STREET, MARITZBURG.

HENRY HOLDGATE

(Formerly with W. E. BALE, Esq.),

Conveyancer, House, Estate, and Financial Agent.

Equitable Fire and Accident Office, Ltd., of Manchester, England.

Secretary to the Union, Responsible, Electric, and Diamond Jubilee Building Societies.

Rents and Accounts Collected; Loans Negotiated; Deeds, Bonds, Wills, Agreements, &c., drawn at the Shortest Notice.

OFFICES: FORESTERS' HALL,
PIETERMARITZ STREET,
MARITZBURG, NATAL.

xxv.

W. J. BELL,

Nurseryman, Florist, and Seedsman.

FLOWER SEEDS, VEGETABLE SEEDS,
            FARM SEEDS, TREE SEEDS.
BULBS, ROSES, FLOWERING SHRUBS,
            ORNAMENTAL SHRUBS AND TREES, ETC.
SOUTH AFRICAN BULBS AND SEEDS.
COLLECTIONS SUPPLIED FROM 10/-, 15/-, 20/-, AND UPWARDS.

SEED STORE : 198, CHURCH STREET.

NURSERIES :

THE VINERY, LOOP STREET,

AND

TOWN BUSH VALLEY,

PIETERMARITZBURG, NATAL.

HESSEY ALLANSON,

CHEMIST AND DRUGGIST,

THE CITY DRUG STORE

Church Street,

OPPOSITE TOWN HALL,

PIETERMARITZBURG.

Dealer in Drugs, Patent Medicines, Toilet Requisites, Photographic Goods, Homœopathic Medicines, &c.

PRESCRIPTIONS CAREFULLY DISPENSED.
LICENSED TO RETAIL METHYLATED SPIRIT. ATTENDANCE AT NIGHT.

THOMAS CHAPLIN,

BUILDER AND CONTRACTOR,

327   CHURCH STREET, MARKET SQUARE   327.

PIETERMARITZBURG.

Building Materials of every Description kept in Stock,
AT LOWEST RATES.

CARPENTRY AND JOINERY WORKS.
Sawing and Planing by Steam at Shortest Notice.
WINDOWS AND DOORS, ETC., ETC.
Estimates given for all kinds of Building.

327   *Church Street, Market Square,*   327.

Stantial & Allerston,

WHOLESALE AND RETAIL 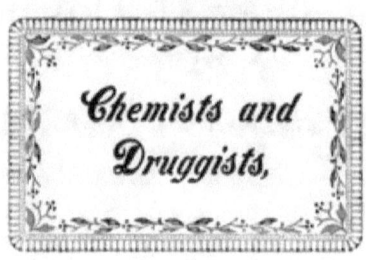 *Chemists and Druggists,*

PIETERMARITZBURG, NATAL.

MANUFACTURERS OF THE

Genuine Natal Lemon Squash.

DEALERS IN

PHOTOGRAPHIC GOODS, APPARATUS, AND SUNDRIES.

The Oldest Established House for DUTCH MEDICINES.

Price Lists on Application.

ADAMS & CO.,

BOOKSELLERS, STATIONERS,
AND NEWS AGENTS,

241, CHURCH STREET, MARITZBURG, AND WEST STREET, DURBAN.

School Books and Requisites as used in the Schools.
Artists' Goods in great variety.
New Books by each Mail Steamer.

ADAMS & CO., 241, CHURCH STREET, PIETERMARITZBURG

THE OLDEST-ESTABLISHED HOUSE IN NATAL.

Thompson & Sons,

Wholesale and Retail Butchers,

COMMERCIAL ROAD & CHURCH STREET,
PIETERMARITZBURG,
WEST STREET AND GREY STREET,
DURBAN.

BUYERS OF FAT STOCK FOR CASH.

Arrangements have been made for a constant supply of Imported Meats.

Contractors to Imperial Government, Colonial Government, Colonial Forces, Indian Immigration Board, Harbour Board, etc., etc.

ROBT. GUY,
281, CHURCH STREET, MARITZBURG,

Contractor to the Imperial and Colonial Governments.

WINES AND SPIRITS of all descriptions. Bass Ale. Guinness' Stout. The celebrated **Bailie Nicol Jarvie Whisky** and **BB Ale. Cigars,** all descriptions.

OILMAN'S STORES of every description at Current Prices.

HARDWARE.—Nails, Screws, Locks, Sash Fasteners, Bolts, Hinges, **White Lead,** Paints, Oils, Bar Iron, Bolts and Nuts, Coach Screws, **Rigby's Axles—all sizes,** Buckets, Shovels, Picks, Mattocks, Steel—all sizes, Trek Chains, Reim Chains, Tumblers—all sizes, Wine Glasses, Claret Glasses, &c., &c.

Indents for any class of Goods executed on best terms.

ROBT. GUY.

ROBERT JONES,
❖ DIRECT ❖ IMPORTER. ❖
❖ GENERAL ❖ MERCHANT. ❖

Large selections of Drapery, Hosiery, Outfitting, Boots, Shoes, and Fancy Goods.

GROCER AND TEA DEALER.

All kinds of Colonial Produce Bought and Sold.

STEAM SAW MILLS AND MEALIE MILLS.

AGENT FOR { Quibell's Famous Sheep Dips.
P. B. Findlay's Imported Carriages.
South African Mutual Life Assurance Society.

ROBERT JONES, UNIVERSAL PROVIDER,
THE STORE, HOWICK.

MASON and BROADBENT,

Ironmongers, &c.,

GENERAL IMPORTERS,

287, CHURCH STREET

(OPPOSITE TOWN HALL).

PIETERMARITZBURG.

xxxi.

WIRE. "STACEY." TELEPHONE 114.

A. J. STACEY & CO.,
221, COMMERCIAL ROAD,
PIETERMARITZBURG, NATAL,

Wholesale and Retail Tobacconists

✦ ✦   AND CIGAR MERCHANTS.

THE BEST-ASSORTED STOCK OF CIGARS AND TOBACCOS IN THE COLONY.

~~~~~~~~~~~~~~~~~~~~~~~~~~~~~~~~~~

W. WATSON ROBERTSON,
Photographer, Chapel Street,
Pietermaritzburg.

By Special Appointment to His Excellency the Governor of Natal.

xxxii.

THE GROSVENOR,

234, LOOP STREET,

PIETERMARITZBURG.

PRIVATE BOARDING HOUSE.

GOOD TABLE.

SMOKING ROOM.

SHOWER BATHS.

Proprietress: Mrs. H. WATKINS.

C. E. TAUNTON,
Public Accountant.
Agent, Conveyancer.

Agent for Union Steamship Company.
  „   African United Insurance Corporation.
  „   Economic Life Insurance Company.
Secretary to The Jubilee Gold Company, Limited.
Auditor to The Natal Bank, Limited.
  „   The City and Suburban Gold Company, Limited.
  „   The Stanhope Gold Mining Company, Limited.
  „   Moodie's G.M. and Exploration Company, Limited.
  „   Salisbury G.M. Company, Limited.
  „   Pietermaritzburg Botanic Society.

Telegraphic Address: "TAUNTON."   Postal Address: BOX 125.

TIMBER STREET, PIETERMARITZBURG.

J. CALVERT & SONS,

Printers, Bookbinders,

and

Engravers,

13 AND 15, PRINTING OFFICE STREET,

PIETERMARITZBURG.

HIGH-CLASS WORK AT REASONABLE PRICES.

R. McALISTER & SONS,

BUILDERS AND CONTRACTORS,

Estimates given for all kinds of Building Work.
General Importers of Builders' Requisites.
Goods Imported on Commission.

MESSRS. R. McALISTER & SONS having an extensive connection and many years' experience in every department of their business, can guarantee the fullest satisfaction to all entrusting business to them.

R. McAlister & Sons, 10, CLUB STREET,
OR P.O. BOX 47

TANKS ! TANKS ! TANKS !

Wilson's Australian (For Mealies and Water)

TWO FIRST-CLASS CERTIFICATES.

G. WILSON, No. 2, WILSON STREET, PIETERMARITZBURG,

PLUMBER AND GENERAL SHEET METAL WORKER,

NEXT TO NATAL BREWERY.

Call and Inspect **J. ANDERSON & CO.'S** Large Stock of **Pipes, Walking Sticks, Cigars, and Tobaccos** before going elsewhere.

We have just unpacked a Large Assortment of **Pipes and Cigars.**

Note Address—

J. ANDERSON & CO.,
❄ TOBACCONISTS, ❄
272, LONGMARKET STREET (Opposite Police Station.)

MARITZBURG CYCLE COMPANY.

Bicycles for Sale on the Hire Purchase System, or for Hire by the Hour, Day, Week, or Month on reasonable terms.
Cycling Taught by an experienced Tutor. Special attention to Ladies. Charges moderate, or free to purchasers of Machines.
Repairs of every description by Experienced Workmen.
The Largest and most complete Stock of Accessories in Natal, including the Latest Novelties. Fresh Supplies constantly arriving.

MARITZBURG CYCLE CO., 264, LONGMARKET STREET.

JAMES & SON,
IMPORTERS OF

Wall Papers, Fancy Goods, Toys and Dolls, Perambulators, Mail Carts, Baskets, Brushes, Games.

LONDON HOUSE, 203 & 205, CHURCH STREET, PIETERMARITZBURG.

WE WORK FOR ALL—

Yirrell & Liggett, 124, CHURCH STREET, MARITZBURG, NATAL.

Cycle Depot: Carriage and Ricksha Works. Cycle Repairs of every kind and description. Agents for the best make of Cycle only. Coach Builders and Manufacturers of Plain and Ornamental Iron Work, etc. Carriages Retrimmed and Painted. Large Stock of Accessories, Cycle Parts, and Fittings.

WE WORK OURSELVES.

W. E. BALE & MORTIMER
(Formerly W. E. BALE),
ESTABLISHED 1849.] [ESTABLISHED 1849.

House, Estate, and Financial Agents.

AGENTS FOR THE
ROYAL INSURANCE COMPANY.

129, ✦ CHURCH ✦ STREET.

De Natal Afrikaner,
PROPRIETORS: J. HERSHENSOHNN & SON.

The only Dutch Newspaper in the Colony, issued twice Weekly.

Circulated all over the Colony, the South African Republic, Free State, and Proviso B, Zululand.

The best Advertising medium for those who wish to advertise for Dutch Custom all over South-East Africa.

Central Photographic Studio,
168, CHAPEL STREET,
MARITZBURG, NATAL, S.A.

JOHN W. CONEY,
Portrait and Landscape Photographer.

High-class work finished in SILVER, PLATINOTYPE, and BROMIDE. Only the Best Materials used.

CABINETS from 25s. per dozen.

IMPERIALS from £2 10s. per dozen.

Special Quotations for 12 x 10 Groups.

Permanent PLATINO-BROMIDE Enlargements.

Every description of Out-door Work executed promptly, with the best results.

Views of Natal always in Stock.

An inspection solicited.

W. HAY,

Baker and Confectioner,

239, CHURCH STREET,

PIETERMARITZBURG.

LAWES & CO.,

MILLERS AND PRODUCE DEALERS,

City Steam Mill,

PRINTING OFFICE STREET, MARITZBURG.

THE PIETERMARITZBURG
STEAM DYEING AND CLEANING WORKS,
ESTABLISHED 1895.

Every description of Ladies' and Gent.'s Garments Cleaned, Dyed, and Pressed.

Having had nine Years' experience with J. PULLAR & SONS, Perth, Dyers and Cleaners to Her Majesty the Queen. Customers may rely on satisfactory Workmanship. Terms, Cash on delivery.

Prices to suit the times.

JAMES WEDDELL, 211, PIETERMARITZ STREET, Pietermaritzburg.

Munro Bros.,

PRINTERS, BOOKBINDERS, AND PUBLISHERS

186, LONGMARKET STREET, MARITZBURG.

Sole Agents for WESTLEY RICHARDS TARGET RIFLES, Verniers, Ventometers, Orthopetics, &c., always on hand.

D. NICOLSON,

BUILDER AND TIMBER MERCHANT,

Contractor to the Imperial Government.

A LARGE AND WELL-ASSORTED STOCK OF

BUILDING MATERIALS

OF ALL DESCRIPTIONS.

**DEALS, PITCH PINE, FLOORING,
CEILING, GALVANISED IRON, &c., &c.
DOORS, WINDOWS,
SKIRTING, MOULDING.**

Estimates given for Buildings of any description.

Sawing, Planing, &c., by Steam Power, at Moderate Charges.

CITY STEAM SAW MILLS,

319, *Church Street,*

PIETERMARITZBURG.

G. H. WILKINSON & CO.
194, ✦ COMMERCIAL ✦ ROAD,

Sixty paces from the Town Hall Tower, Maritzburg,

Supply *NATIVE BULBS* and *Seeds, Timber and Ornamental Trees, Fruit Trees, Camellias, Azaleas, Roses,* and other *Flowering Shrubs.* Seed Potatoes commence to arrive from England in November, and Seed from these is supplied in Winter and Spring.

H. T. PEACH.
Furniture, Curio, and *General Dealer,*
231, COMMERCIAL ROAD,
PIETERMARITZBURG.

LIVERPOOL HOUSE.
ROBERT ELLIOT,
Grocer, Tea Blender, and Italian Warehouseman,

Has a Large and Well-assorted Stock in the above lines. Fresh Goods constantly arriving.

Having had a large Home experience in the Tea Trade, is making a leading feature of this Branch, and solicits a trial of his Special Blends. All Orders, Town and Country, receive prompt personal attention.

ROBERT ELLIOT, **189, Church Street, Maritzburg**
(Next door to the Golden Boot).

E. G. KERBY & CO.,
191, Church Street, Maritzburg,
Watch & Clock Makers, Silversmiths, Jewellers, Etc.

Diamonds. Precious Stones. Optical Goods.
A Large Stock of Articles specially selected for Presentation.

JESSE SMITH & SON,
STATUARIES AND MASONS,
BUILDERS AND CONTRACTORS,
STEAM MARBLE & STONE WORKS
(ESTABLISHED 1850,)

COMMERCIAL ROAD, MARITZBURG,
WEST STREET (WEST), DURBAN, and
De KORTE STREET, JOHANNESBURG.

Importers of all kinds of Marble and Granite, in Chimney Pieces, Cemetery Memorials, etc.

Designs and Estimates forwarded on Application.

FISHER, PRIOR & WEDDELL,
Nursery Seedsmen & Floral Artists,
151, CHURCH STREET.

Tested Farm Seeds.
Tested Vegetable Seeds.
Tested Flower Seeds.

All description of Trees, Plants and Shrubs, Bouquets Wreaths and Crosses, made up on the Shortest Notice.

Winners of the Silver Cup for Roses, 1897; First-Class Certificate for Agricultural Seeds, 1897; Certificate of Merit for Floral Devices, 1897.

Descriptive Catalogue on application.

Mr. John M. Hershensohnn,
CAPE UNIVERSITY,
Sworn Translator of the English and Dutch Languages,

201, Burger Street, Maritzburg.

STANDARD RESTUARANT & NATAL CLUB,
CHURCH STREET,
PIETERMARITZBURG.

Proprietor: C. WOODHOUSE.

J. CONEY,
The City Undertaker,
162, CHAPEL STREET, MARITZBURG.

Polished Oak and Panelled Coffins at Shortest Notice.

N.B.—HEARSE AND MOURNING COACH FOR HIRE.

S. W. LEAKE,
Wholesale and Retail
STATIONER, PRINTER, AND BOOKSELLER
'CITY' RUBBER STAMP MAKER,

Direct Importer of

Tennis, Cricket, and other Game Requisites,
275, CHURCH STREET (opposite Town Hall), MARITZBURG.

ROBT. A. DIX,
Accountant, Conveyancer, Financial, and General Agent,
Borough Auditor, Maritzburg.

Agent for the Alliance Assurance Company, of London.

LYLE'S CHAMBERS,   P.O. BOX No. 76
250, Church Street, Pietermaritzburg.

[Established 1854.] [Established 1854.]

W. W. WATLING, WATCHMAKER, JEWELLER, AND OPTICIAN, 178, CHURCH STREET, MARITZBURG.

A Nice Stock of Watches, Jewellery, and Spectacles for Sale.
Goods sent on approbation.
Country Orders carefully attended to.
All work guaranteed.

Wm. Laws Caney,
PHOTOGRAPHER,
Studio, Opposite Natal Bank.

J. W. DE HAAS,
COMMISSION AGENT,
Stall No. 6, Market Hall,
Maritzburg, Natal.

VICTORIA HOTEL
(LATE DIAMOND),
TIMBER AND LONGMARKET STREETS,
PIETERMARITZBURG.

This Old-Established House is the most Central Hotel in Town. It has been recently renovated and greatly improved throughout.

SHOWER AND PLUNGE BATHS.

Terms:—7/6 per Day; 42/- per week. Special Terms for Monthly Residents.

TRAINS MET WHEN ADVISED.

R. LAMBERT, Proprietor.

IMPERIAL ✢ HOTEL,

212 & 214, Loop Street,

MARITZBURG.

Proprietress: Mrs. EMMA THRESH.

This is the Largest and Best Hotel in the City. It is Centrally situated, near the Principal Business part of the Town, the Theatre, and the Park, being convenient for Business men as well as those who come on pleasure.

The Hotel is fitted throughout with Electric Light and other modern conveniences.

A Bus meets all Trains.

**Telegraphic Address: "IMPERIAL."
P.O. BOX 140.**

H. DOIDGE,
Y.M.C.A. BUILDINGS,
LONGMARKET ✦ STREET,
BOOKSELLER AND STATIONER.

Bibles, Religious Literature,
Books, Wall Texts, Etc.

Robert Fuller, Chemist and Druggist,
MANUFACTURER OF HIGH-CLASS MINERAL WATERS.
268, LONGMARKET STREET, and
73, CHURCH STREET, MARITZBURG.

Direct Importer of Pure Drugs, Chemicals, Patent and Homœopathic Medicines, Perfumery, Sponges, Toilet Requisites, etc., etc.

N.B.—Prescriptions accurately dispensed. Night Bells promptly attended to.

L. W. ODELL, TIMBER MERCHANT, GENERAL IRONMONGER,

Deals, Pine and Poplar Boards, Doors, Windows, Ceiling, Flooring, and Cement.

Window Glass, Nails, Oils, Paints, and Paraffin, at lowest Prices. Send for Quotations.

184, CHURCH STREET, PIETERMARITZBURG.

COLONIAL INDUSTRY.
JOHN HUGHES,
CABINETMAKER AND UPHOLSTERER,

Manufacturer of Furniture suitable for Mansion or Cottage, from Colonial and Imported Wood.

147 AND 149, CHURCH STREET, PIETERMARIIZBURG.

GEO. SMITH,

WATCH AND CLOCKMAKER,
JEWELLER AND SILVERSMITH,

171, CHURCH STREET, PIETERMARITZBURG.

Studs, Sleeve Links, Scarf Pins, Lockets, Brooches, Earrings, Dress Rings, Keepers.

Every description of Repairs to Watches, Clocks, Jewellery, Optical and Scientific Instruments, Musical Boxes, &c., promptly and properly executed.

Electric Gilding and Silver Plating done on the Premises.

R. H. COOPER,

Contractor and Builder,

Contractor to Natal Government Railways.

ALL KINDS OF CONTRACT WORK UNDERTAKEN.

ESTIMATES GIVEN FOR ALL KINDS OF BUILDING WORK.

293, Pietermaritz Street,

Pietermaritzburg, Natal.

H. COLLINS,

TIMBER MERCHANT, BUILDER AND CONTRACTOR.

Staircases, Store Fronts, Fittings, and Joinery of every description made to Order at Shortest Notice. Special Terms to the Trade.

Wood and Iron Buildings, Etc., and all Buildings at Lowest Rates.

ADDRESS:

H. COLLINS,
Club and Pietermaritz Streets,
Pietermaritzburg

SCHWAKE, WATT & CO.,

Established 1878.

LONGMARKET ST.,

Near Plough Hotel,

Market Square.

All work and Repairs Guaranteed, and done by Experienced Workmen.

Three Years' Guarantee.

WATCHMAKERS, JEWELLERS, AND OPTICIANS.

This well-known Firm keeps a Superior and Selected Stock of Gold and Silver Watches, Alberts, Diamond, Engagement and other Rings; Gold and Silver Brooches, Silver and Electro-plate of best quality, Cutlery, and Hollow Ground Razors; Scissors of Superior make; all requisites in the Optical Line, such as Field Glasses, Telescopes, etc.; Gold, Silver, Nickel, and Steel Spectacles and Folders; Cylindrical and Cataract Lenses made to Order; Oculists' formulas accurately carried out.

J. H. GODDARD,

Builder and Contractor,

101, BOSHOFF STREET,

MARITZBURG.

All kinds of Contract Work undertaken.
Estimates given on application.

R. MASON & SON,
ESTABLISHED
THE CORN EXCHANGE
IN 1868.

And have for many Years held, and still hold, the PREMIER Position in the City as

GRAIN MERCHANTS AND MILLERS.

Business Premises : 303, *Church Street.*

MILLS (Water-power), situated on the Umsindusi River, Edendale Road.

ADDRESS—
**R. MASON & SON,
303, Church Street,
Maritzburg, Natal.**

Telegraph: "SOWERSBY," Maritzburg.

www.ingramcontent.com/pod-product-compliance
Lightning Source LLC
Chambersburg PA
CBHW031351230426
43670CB00006B/508